Elizabeth City County Virginia

DEED ABSTRACTS

1787–1800

Joan Charles

HERITAGE BOOKS
2012

HERITAGE BOOKS
AN IMPRINT OF HERITAGE BOOKS, INC.

Books, CDs, and more—Worldwide

For our listing of thousands of titles see our website
at
www.HeritageBooks.com

Published 2012 by
HERITAGE BOOKS, INC.
Publishing Division
100 Railroad Ave. #104
Westminster, Maryland 21157

Copyright © 1994 Joan Charles

Other Heritage Books by the author:
Elizabeth City County, Virginia Deed Abstracts, 1787–1800
Elizabeth City County, Virginia Wills, 1733–1799
Elizabeth City County, Virginia Wills, 1800–1859

All rights reserved. No part of this book may be reproduced or transmitted in any form or by any means, electronic or mechanical, including photocopying, recording or by any information storage and retrieval system without written permission from the author, except for the inclusion of brief quotations in a review.

International Standard Book Numbers
Paperbound: 978-1-55613-983-3
Clothbound: 978-0-7884-9117-7

Elizabeth City County, Virginia 1787-1800

TABLE OF CONTENTS

```
Preface..........................................v
Acknowledgements..............................vii
How to Use This Book.........................viii
Table of Contents - Deed Book............1 - 13
Deed Book 34...........................15 - 115
Index - All Name......................117 - 157
Index of Places.......................159 - 162
```

Elizabeth City County, Virginia 1787-1800

PREFACE

Elizabeth City County was one of the early counties of Virginia and the City of Hampton, which now incoroporates the land mass of Elizabeth City County is considered the oldest, continuous, English-speaking settlement in the United States dating from 1610.

It is hoped this book will be a welcomed research tool for genealogists, historians, and archaeologists.

Deed Book 34 is located in the Hampton Circuit Courthouse in Hampton, Virginia. It is an original handwritten volume of 523 pages and includes deeds, probate of wills, appraisement of estates, and miscellaneous documents.

The abstracts include all names from each document as well as place names and their description if included in the original text. The last item was included for future reference of archaeologists in particular.

The abstracts are in their simplest form and include type of transaction, names, dates and the name of the Clerk of Court when known.

Deed Book 34 contains a wealth of information about the county at the end of the 18th century. Estate appraisements as well as estate accountings give generous clues to the life-style and economy of the area. Many of the deeds well define the parcels of land with surveyor's measurements and landmarks.

Elizabeth City County, Virginia 1787-1800

ACKNOWLEDGEMENTS

I would particularly like to thank Juanita Gupton, the present Clerk of Court for the Circuit Court of Hampton, for allowing me access to Deed Book 34. I would also like to thank all the people who supported me in this effort and put up with my "intensity" during the work.

Elizabeth City County, Virginia 1787-1800

HOW TO USE THIS BOOK

This book is in a very simple format. Please keep in mind that the index is numbered by the page or folio of the original deed book and not by the number of the page on which it appears in this book. **Bold numbers** indicate documents of which the person was a major party or that person's will.

Elizabeth City County, Virginia 1787-1800

DEED BOOK 34

TABLE OF CONTENTS

Note: Numbers are in reference to the
pages in the original Court Book

1-2	Will - John Armisteade
2.	Obligation Bond - Westwood, Parsons, King for Westwood as Sheriff
3.	Obligation Bond - Westwood, Parsons, King for Westwood as Sheriff
3.	Obligation Bond - Westwood, Parsons, King for Westwood as Sheriff
4-5	Deed/land - Herbert/Jennings
5-7	Appraisement of Estate - John Weymouth
7-9	Account of Estate - John Smelt
9-10	Appraisement of Estate - Robert Wellings
10.	Deed/land - Pool/Cooper
11.	Deed/land - Pool/Bayley
11-12	Deed/land - Cowper/Pool
12.	Deed/land - King/Latimer
13.	Deed/lot - Parish/Harper
13.	Hampton Warehouse Accounts
14.	Sale of slaves - Jones,Redmon/Brough
14-15	Account of Estate - Rosea Latimer
15-15a	Deed/land - Cary/Maddisson
15a-16	Deed/land - Fields/Armistead
16-18	Deed/land - Armistead/Burk
18-19	Deed/land - Barron,King/Selden
19-20	Will - James Bray Armistead
20-21	Will - Ann Wilson
21-22	Appraisement of Estate - Westwood Armistead
23.	Account of Estate - Robert Willings
24.	Division of slaves - Westwood Armistead Estate
24-25	Sale of slaves - Jones, Redmon, Redman/Brough
25-26	Deed/land - Wallace/King
26-27	Deed/land - Smith/Armistead
28.	Deed/land - Minson/Stores
29.	Account of Estate - Simon Hollier

Elizabeth City County, Virginia 1787-1800

30.	Appraisement of Estate - James B. Armistead
31-33	Account of Estate - Thomas Skinner
33-34	Deed/land - Minson/Jennings
34-35	Acknowledgement of sale - Mary Herbert
36.	Appraisement of Estate - John Armistead
37.	Deed/lot - Pauls, Johnson/Westwood
38.	Deed/lot - Wood/Harper
39.	Deed/lot - Harper/Wood
40-41	Deed/lot - Wood/Harper
41.	Sale of slaves - Booker/Brough
42.	Sale of slaves - Cotton/Brough
43-45	Deed/land - Cunningham/Hope
45-46	Deed/lot - Pasteur/Buxton
46-47	Deed/land,slaves - Ross/King
48.	Will - Thomas Wooten
49.	Deed/land - Herbert/Hope
50.	Deed/land - King/Moore
51.	Deed/land - Jenkins/Sands
52.	Deed/land - Moore/King
53.	Deed/land - Cary for Hollier/Hollier
54-55	Deed/land - Wooten/Henderson
55-56	Deed/land - Dewbre/Davis
56.	Deed/lot - Westwood/Wallace
57.	Deed/lot - Lacklin/Barron
58.	Sale of slave - Paine/Bayley
58-59	Release - Selden/Hatton
60.	Receipt for slaves - Bowery
61-62	Deed/land - Westwood/Armistead
62.	Sale of slaves - Parish/Bowery
63.	Sale of slave - Williams/Brough
63.	Gift of slaves - Armistead/Armistead
64.	Will - Dianna Wallace Bayley
65.	Deed/land - Barron/Barron
66-67	Deed/land - Hatton/Cary
68.	Deed/land - Burt/Umphlet
69.	Release - Meredith/Delaney
70-71	Deed/land - Parsons/Wray
71-72	Debt - Thomas Scott/Hope
72-74	Deed/land - Williams/Lewis
75-76	Deed/land - Minson/Bushell
77-78	Deed/land - Minson/Stores
78-79	Account of Estate - James B. Armistead

Elizabeth City County, Virginia 1787-1800

79-80	Account of Estate - Moses Armistead
81.	Deed/lot - Pearse/Westwood
82.	Deed/lot - Westwood/Face
83.	Sale of slaves - Dixon/King
84-85	Will - Wilson Curle
86.	Account of Estate - Moses Armistead
87.	Appraisement of Estate - Ann Wilson
87-88	Account for construction - Bland/Pool
88-92	Appraisement of Estate - John Lowry
93-94	Court case - Bowrey/Chapman
95-96	Deed/land - Lee/Selden
96-97	Deed/land - Elott/Elott (Ellott)
97.	Pre-nuptual agreement - Latimer/Marshall/Selden
98.	Deed/land - Copeland, Allen/King
98.	Release - King/Minson
99.	Deed/land - Mercer/Burke
99.	Release - King/Stores
100.	Account of Estate - Nathaniel Bell
101.	Account of Estate - Nathaniel Bell/William Sandefur
102-105	Account of Estate - Francis Mallory
106.	Sale of slave - Colton/Brough
106.	Deed/land - Humphlet/Daes
107.	Release - King/Minson
107.	Sale of slaves and livestock - Smelt/King
108.	Will - William Gooch
109.	Deed/land - Lee/Martin
109.	Emancipation - Rogers/Lucy
110.	Account of Estate - Robert Brough
110.	Acknowledgement of indenture - Pasteur/Buxton
111-112	Will - Robert Armistead
112-113	Sale of slaves and livestock - Applewhaite/King
113-114	Deed/lot - Hopkin/Hope
114.	Will - Anne Skinner
115-116	Appraisement of Estate - James Marshall
116-117	Appraisement of Slaves - Francis Mallory
118.	Deed/land - Cutiller/Kerby
119.	Will - Frazier Stores

Elizabeth City County, Virginia 1787-1800

120.	Will - Mary Smith
121.	Deed/land - Cunningham/Cunningham
121-122	Deed/land - Cunningham/Cunningham
122.	Deed/land - Watts/Cooper
123.	Deed/land - Westwood/Haughton
123.	Deed/land - Latimer/Latimer
124.	Deed/land - Hurst/Rowland
124.	Power of Attorney - Parcell/Selden
125.	Deed/land - Moore/Moore
126.	Will - Mary Powell
127.	Obligation Bond - Booker,Moore,Brodie for Booker as Sheriff
128.	Obligation Bond - Booker,Moore,Brodie for Booker as Sheriff
128-129	Deed/land - Cooper/Cooper
130.	Sale of slave - Banks/Perry
130-131	Deed/lot - Harper/Tarrant
131-132	Deed/land - Minson/Boutwell
132-133	Deed/land - Baker/King
133-134	Deed/land - Barron/King
134.	Will - John Weymouth
134-135	Appraisement of Estate - Frazer Stores
136.	Will - William Lewis
137.	Deed/land - Bennett/Jennings
138.	Deed/land - Westwood/Wray
139.	Auction of Little Scotland to Roe Cowper
140.	Will - Mark Hall
141.	Division of Estate - Frazer Stores
141-142	Account of Estate - Frazer Stores
142.	Division of Slaves - Westwood/King/Bayley
143-144	Deed/land - Brough/McCan
144.	Settlement of Estate - Capt. John Harris
145-146	Deed/land - Selden/Page
147-148	Deed/lot - Proby/Armistead
148-149	Deed/land - Jennings/Watts
150.	Sale of slaves - Armistead/Armistead
150.	Sale of slave - Armistead/Armistead
151.	Sale of slaves - Armistead/Armistead
152-153	Deed/land - Reade for Haynes/Robinson
154.	Will - Thomas Jennings

Elizabeth City County, Virginia 1787-1800

155.	Will - Martha Ross
155-157	Deed/land - Act of Assembly/Hutchings
157.	Deed/land - Williams for Lewis Estate /Lewis
158.	Deed/land - Williams for Lewis Estate /Clark
159-160	Deed/land - Bushell/Cain
160.	Obligation Bond - Wray/Wray/Booker for Wray as Surveyor
161-162	Deed/lots - Foster for King/Williams, Boyce for Bailey
162-163	Deed/lots - Foster/King
164-165	Deed/land - King/Carbier
166.	Letter of Expatriation - James Parsons
167-168	Appraisement of Estate - Deana Wallace Bailey
168.	Appraisement of Estate - Paul Carbier
169.	Deed/lot - Armistead/Meredith
170.	Deed/lot - King/Borrowdale
171.	Deed/land - Curle/Jennings
172.	Will - Mary Latimer
173-174	Deed/land - Meredith/Armistead
175-176	Deed/land - Westwood/Finnie
176-177	Sale of slaves - Watts
177.	Will - Charles Bayley
178-179	Deed/lot - Borrowdale/King
179-181	Deed/land - Poole/Latimer
182.	Deed/lot - William & Mary College/Armistead
183.	Deed/land - King/King
183-184	Gift of slaves - Manice/Bowery
184-185	Deed/tripartite - Ward/Bowery/Brough
185-187	Deed/lot - Brough/Bowery
188.	Deed/land - Wallace/Latimer
189-190	Deed/land - Williams,Boyce for Armistead / King
190-191	Obligation Bond - Armistead/Hope
191-194	Deed/land - Cary/Hope
194-196	Deed/lots - Selden/Meredith
197.	Deed/land - Dixon/Backhouse
198-200	Deed/land - Borrowdale/Jones (for boat Charles)
201-202	Deed/lot - Barron/Hope
202-203	Deed/land - Latimer/Hope

Elizabeth City County, Virginia 1787-1800

```
204-205  Deed/lot - Cowper/Hope
205-206  Deed/land - Mallory/Mallory
206-207  Deed/land - Wellings/Wilson
207-208  Deed/land - King/Bains
209-210  Deed/land - Corbier,King/Sheppard
211.     Deed/land - Seymour/Westwood,
         Wooten, Dunn
211-212  Deed/lot - Banks/Poole
213-214  Deed/land - Pasteur/Pollard
214-215  Will - Barbara Jones
216.     Bond of Debt - Yancey/Henderson
216-217  Sale of slaves - Smith/Hoomes
217-218  Sale of slave - Bowrey/Brough
218-219  Deed/land - Bowrey/Brough
220.     Will - Mary Randle
220-221  Will - Robert Smelt
221-222  Will - Thomas Humphlet
222.     Will - Johnson Ross
223.     Will - Rebecca Dewbre
224.     Deed/land - Yancey/Wash
224-225  Power of Attorney - Yancey to Duke
225.     Will - Archelaus Yancey
226.     Will - Arthur Henderson
227-230  Account of Estate - John Reade
231-233  Deed/land - Powell/Cowper
233-234  Deed/land - Reade/Purdie
234-235  Deed/lot - King/Westwood
235-237  Deed/land - Westwood/Westwood
237-238  Will - Augustine Moore
238-239  Will - Hunter
240-241  Appraisement of Estate - Rebecca
         Dewbre
241.     Appraisement of Estate - Gerrard
         Seymour
242-243  Deed/land - Cowper/Payne
243-244  Deed/lot - Westwood/Bates
245-246  Rental agreement - Jenkins/Burkette
246.     Will - Judy Saunders
247-248  Will - John Cary
248-249  Deed/land - Westwood/King
249-250  Sale of slaves - Armistead/Allen
250.     Will - Johnson Tabb
251.     Will - Nathaniel Whitaker
252.     Deed/land and slaves in trust -
```

Elizabeth City County, Virginia 1787-1800

	Page/King
253.	Receipt for slaves, property - Sheriff/Brough
253-254	Appraisement of Estate - Robert Armistead
255-257	Sale of Estate - Robert Armistead
258-259	Inventory of Estate - Barbara Jones
260.	Appraisement of Estate - Archelus Yancey
261-262	Deed/land - Moore/Moore
263-265	Power of Attorney - Blane/Young
266-267	Deed/lot - Jennings, Jennings, Jennings/Hope
267-268	Deed/lot - Wallace/Parish
269.	Deed/land - Jiggetts/Burk
270-272	Deed/land - Rowland/Parish
272-273	Deed/land - Wray/Wray
273-274	Deed/land - Wray/Wray
275-276	Deed/lot - Face/Hurst
276-277	Deed/land - Parish/Wallace
277-278	Deed/land - Parsons/Greenhow
279.	Deed/land - Westwood,Westwood/King
280.	Sale of slaves and livestock - Brough/Brough
280-281	Sale of slave - Manice/Robert Brough
281-282	Sale of slaves - Manice/Brough
282-283	Deed/land - Stores/Stores
283-284	Sale of slaves - Burt/Humphlet,Minson
284-285	Articles of Agreement of possession of slaves - Humphlet/Minson
285.	Settlement of estate of James Bayley
286.	Appraisal and division of slaves of John Bayley's estate
287.	Receipt for sale of slaves - Westwood/Redwood
287.	Will - John Stores
288.	Will - Job Colton
289.	Appraisement of Estate - Chevers Elliott
289.	Account of Sale of Estate - Elizabeth Russell
290.	Appraisement of Estate - James Williams
291.	Account of Estate - James Stores

Elizabeth City County, Virginia 1787-1800

291.	Appraisement of Estate - John Wilson, Jr.
292-293	Sales of Estate - John Wilson
293-294	Deed/lot - Wray/Wray
294-295	Deed/lot - Selden/Meredith
296.	Will - Ann Jones
297-298	Will - Mary Tarrant
298.	Will - Hannah King
299-300	Deed/land - Cowper/Green
300-301	Deed/land - Paine/Green
302.	Receipt for payment - Jones/Borrowdale
302-303	Deed/lot - Harper/Harper
304.	Appraisement of Estate - John Robinson
305-306	Deed/land - Dobson/King
307.	Gifts - Ottley/his children
308.	Sale of slaves - Manice/Bowry
309.	Will - Edward Delaney
309-310	Will - Robert Elliott
311-312	Will - Francis Riddlehurst
313-314	Deed/lot - Brodie/Street
314.	Deed/land - King/Face
315-316	Deed/lot - Westwood/Face
317.	Acknowledgement of sale - Wallace/Parish
318.	Deed/lot - Hicks/Rogers
318.	Court order of audit of records
319-320	Deed/lot - Hutchings/King,Booker - trustees
320-321	Deed/land - King/King
322-323	Obligation Bond - Armistead, Armistead, King for R. Armistead as Sheriff
323.	Receipt for payment from estate - Sandefer/Sheriff
324.	Account of Estate - William Badgitt
325.	Will - Mary Tabb
326.	Obligation Bond - Jones, Herbert for Jones as Coronor
326-327	Deed/land - Latimer/Latimer
327-328	Deed/land - Baker/King
329.	Deed/land - Williams/Routen
330-331	Deed/land - Allen/King
331-333	Deed/lot - McClurg,Smith,King/Westwood
333-334	Sale of slaves - Brough/Colton

Elizabeth City County, Virginia 1787-1800

334.	Sale of slaves - Colton/Brough
335.	Deed/land - Dewbre/Davis
336.	Deed/land - Latimer/King
337.	Deed/land - Latimer/Dewbre
338.	Appraisement of Estate - James Tompkins
338.	Will - John Daws
339.	Lease - Jennings for Robinson/Minson
339-340	Appraisement of Estate - Capt. John Hunter
341.	Deed/land - Reade/Purdie
342-343	Account of Sale of Estate - Rebecca Dewbry
343.	Power of Attorney - Walker/Wray
344-345	Deed/land - Wray for Walker/Jennings
345-346	Settlement of Estate - Rebecca Dewbry
347-348	Deed/land - Jennings/Wray
348.	Deed of gift of lot - Banks/Banks
349.	Will - Thomas Kerby
349.	Will - William Goddin
350-351	Deed/lease of land - Jenkins/Smelt
351.	Emancipation - Cooper/Jack
352.	Deed/lot - Pauls/Pauls
353.	Will - Benjamin Bryan
353-354	Deed/land - Moore/Moore
355.	Deed/land - Paine/Been
356-358	Deed/lot - Meredith/Armistead
358.	Deed/land - Armistead/Westwood
359-360	Account of Sale of Estate - Richard Dixon
360-361	Account of Sale of Estate - Francis Pool
362.	Account of Sale of Estate - James and Judy Sanders
363-364	Deed/lot - Ward/Brough/Brough
364-365	Deed/land - Latimer/Davis
365.	Will (Noncupative) - John Bright
366.	Sale of slaves - Moore/Moore/Moore
366-368	Deed/land - Wallace/Allen
368-369	Deed/land - Wray/Wray
369-371	Deed/land - Davis/Lowry
371-372	Deed/land - Cooper for Watts/Cooper
372-373	Mortage of possessions - Applewhaite/King

Elizabeth City County, Virginia 1787-1800

373-374	Appraisement of Estate - James Bayley
374.	Appraisement of Estate - John Bayley
375.	Deed/lot - Boush/Rogers
376.	Will - Jean Watts
376-377	Deed/lot - Wray/Page
377-379	Petition of writ ad quod Damnum - Robert Armistead
380-382	Account of Estate - Moss Armistead
383.	Will - Joseph Meredith
383-384	Will - Fanny Smith
384.	Sale of slaves - Wray/Brough
385-386	Deed/lot - Page/Jones
386-387	Receipt for horses to cover debt - Allen/Face
387-388	Will - Casar Tarrant
388-389	Acknowledgement of sale of land - Westwood/Bates
389-390	Deed/land - Cowper/King
390.	Appraisement of Estate - Samuel Bland
391.	Accounting of Estate - James Tompkins
391.	Sale of Estate - William Godwin (Goddin)
392.	Account of Sale of Estate - Frazer Stores
392-393	Account of Sale of Estate - William Watkins
393-394	Deed/land and slaves - Bayley/Jones
395-399	PAGES ARE BLANK
400-401	Deed/lot - Barron/Bedenfield
401-402	Power of Attorney - Yancey/Yancey
402.	Release of debt - Wray for Walker/Jennings
403.	Deed/land - King for Henderson/Muray
404.	Deed/lot - Westwood/Watts
405-406	Deed/land - Pasteur/Ham (Hame,Hamm)
406-407	Will - Nathaniel Bedingfield
407-408	Will - J. Thomas Silverthorn
409-410	Will - Samuel Watts
410-411	Will - John Banes (Baines)
411-412	Division of Slaves - James Bayley
412-413	Deed/house,slaves,goods for debt - Minson/King
414-415	Deed/land for debt - Davis/King
415-416	Deed/land - King/Armistead

Elizabeth City County, Virginia 1787-1800

416-417	Appraisement of Estate - Joseph Meredith
417-418	Account of Estate - William M. Holland
419.	Sale of slaves - Manson/Brough
420.	Deed/land - Armistead/Allen
421-422	Deed/land - Thomas/Williams
423-424	Deed/lot - Pierce/Hopkins
425.	Acknowledgement of sale - Charity Harper
426-427	Deed/land - Lattimer/Howell
427-428	Deed/lots - Whittaker/Westwood
428.	Receipt for payment - Dixon/Backhouse
429-430	Acknowledgement of sale - Ann Dixon
430-431	Appraisement of Estate - Mary Curle
431.	Account of Estate - Col. Francis Mallory
432-435	Account of Estate - Mary Mallory
436-437	Sale of Estate - Col. Francis Mallory, Mary Mallory
438.	Division of Estate - Francis Mallory, Mary Mallory
438.	Deed/lot - Westwood/Westwood
439-440	Deed/lot - Tarrant/Armistead
440.	Sale of slaves - Curle/King
441.	Will - John Williams
442.	Account of Estate - Jno. Weymouth
443.	Deed/land and lot - King/Cary
444.	Acknowledgement of sale - Martha King
445.	Acknowledgement of sale - Martha King
446-447	Deed/land - King/Jones
448.	Will - Merit Moore
449.	Appraisement of estate - Margaret Bell
449-450	Will - Martha Armistead
451-452	Deed/land - Tennis/Armistead
452-453	Deed/land - King,Herbert for Jones/Minson
453.	Gift of slaves - Lattermore (Latimer)/Hains
454.	Deed/land - Armistead, Seymour, Shepard/Tennis
455-456	Deed/land - Banes(Bains)/Davis
456-457	Deed/land - Thomas/Allen
458-459	Deed/land - Shields for Kerby, Marrow, Harwood/Hylton

Elizabeth City County, Virginia 1787-1800

460.	Deed/land - Corbieres,King/Beauregard
461.	Sale of slaves - Moore/Moore
462.	Sale of slave - Elliott/Elliott
462.	Deed of release - King/Minson
463.	Will - James S. Ballard
463.	Deed of release - Wray/Dixon
464.	Mortgage of slaves - King/Boyce
464-465	Sale of slaves - King/Herbert
465.	Deed/land - Poole/King
466.	Deed/goods as security - Cowper/King
467.	Deed/land - Bland/Latimer
468.	Emancipation - Cary/Kate
468.	Protest by Wilson Miles Cary
469-471	Deed/lot - Ward/Brough/Brough
471-472	Deed/land - Beauregard,King/Wallace
472.	Appraisement of Estate - Martha Armistead
473.	Appraisement of Estate - Robert Wallace
474.	Account of Sale of Estate - Robert Wallace
475.	Deed/land - Marrow for Smelt/Parsons
476.	Deed/land - Parsons/Marrow
477.	Will - Waldwin Shephard Morris
477.	Emancipation - Latimer/Sam
478.	Account of Estate - Thomas Jiggetts
479.	Acknowledgement of sale - Ann Bland
480.	Deed/land - Green/Paine
481-482	Will - Robert Sandefer Russell
483.	Deed/land - Selden/Stores
484-485	Deed/land - Allen/Amory
486-487	Will - William Armistead the elder
487.	Will - John Wood
488.	Sale of slaves - King/Moore/King
489.	Release of debt - Brough/Skinner
489-490	Account of Estate - Robert Bright
491.	Account of Estate - Jno. Parsons
492.	Deed/land - Langhorne/Wellings
493.	Bond for debt - Wooten/King
493.	Setting of Dower - Sarah Cunningham
494-495	Deed/lot - Jones/Westwood
495.	Deed/land - Cunningham/Skinner
496.	Bill of sale - Hardyman/Cary
496.	Account of Sales of Estate - Archilus

Elizabeth City County, Virginia 1787-1800

	Yancey
497.	Deed/land - Booker/Fenn
498.	Deed/land - Fenn/Booker
499.	Appraisement of Estate - James Banks
500.	Account of Sales of Estate - James Banks
501.	Deed/land - Mallory/Mallory
502.	Deed/grist mill - Walker/Armistead
503.	Deed/land - Armistead/Armistead
504.	Account of Sales of Estate - Thomas Fenn
505.	Appraisement of Estate - Robert Smelt
506-507	Account of Estate - Robert Smelt
507.	Account of Estate - Archilus Yancey
508.	Appraisement of Estate - Robert Landrum
509.	Account of Sale of Estate - Margaret Bell
510.	Account of Estate - Margaret Bell
510.	Receipt of Court Action - Marrow for Smelt
511.	Deed of Release - King/Cunningham
512.	Will - Peter Fiveash
513.	Deed/land - Skinner/Thomas
514.	Appraisement of Estate - Mark Hall
515-519	Account of Sale of Estate - Robert Smelt
519-520	Will - Jacob Wray
521.	Will - John Curle King
522.	Will - James Berry
522-523	Will - John Skinner
523.	Sale of slave - Kerby/Selden
524.	Acknowledgement of sale - Sarah Cunningham
525.	Sale of slaves - Brough/Brough
526.	Account of Estate - Captain Joseph Meredith
527.	Account of Estate - Martha Armistead
527.	Account of Estate - Thomas Kerby
528-529	Account of Estate - Robert Wallace
530.	Account of Estate - David Saunders
531-532	Writ of Quod Damnum - Commonwealth of Virginia / Sheriff

Elizabeth City County, Virginia 1787-1800

Elizabeth City County, Virginia 1787-1800

DEED BOOK 34

1-2 - **John Armisteade** - March 26, 1787 - Will - March 26, 1787 - Elizabeth Armisteade, wife; John Armisteade, son; Robert Armisteade, son; Thomas Smith, son-in-law. Slaves: Molly, Sarah, Nan, China, Sampson, Grisdal, Aaron, Gum, China Lucy, Fan. Wit: John Cary, George Booker, Michael King, Robert Armistead. January 27, 1791 - recorded:Johnson Tabb.

2 - **Worlick Westwood, William A. Thos. Parsons, Michael King** - January 27, 1791 - Obligation bond to Beverly Randolph, Governor of Virginia - for Worlick Westwood's appointment as Sheriff of Elizabeth City County. January 27, 1791 - recorded:Johnson Tabb.

3 - **Worlick Westwood, William A. Thomas Parsons, Michael King** - January 27, 1791 Obligation bond to Jacquilen Ambler, Treasurer of Virginia - for Worlick Westwood's appointment as Sheriff of Elizabeth City County. Recorded:Johnson Tabb.

3 - **Worlick Westwood, William Moore, William A. Thos. Parsons** - March 25, 1791 - Obligation bond to Beverly Randolph, Governor of Virginia - for Worlick Westwood's appointment as Sheriff of Elizabeth City County. recorded:Johnson Tabb.

4-5 - **Pascow Herbert, mariner and his wife Mary / Thomas Jennings, Jr.** - November 19, 1790 - Indenture for 50 acres: beginning at the River and running an east course along the line of John Robinson's lands to a small red oak, thence running about a northwest course to a white gum near a branch, thence to a black gum near the same course, continuing near the same course on the west side of the branch as the traces are marked to a black gum on the same

Elizabeth City County, Virginia, 1787-1800

side, opposite to Roe Cowper's Saw Pitt at his Wood Landing and running from thence as the branch runs to Cary Selden's Land (as said Selden's land runs over the creek) and from Selden's line a west course to the river and from thence as the river runs to the beginning place. Pascow Herbert purchased land from Francis Tarrant, son of Carter Tarrant (deceased) who purchased the said land of Roe Cooper. Wit: Benjn. Bryan, John Parish, Jr., John Jennings. January 27, 1791 - recorded: Johnson Tabb.

5-7 - **John Weymouth** - December 3, 1787 - Appraisement of estate - Household goods, livestock. Appraisers: Wm. Gooch, Thos. Minson, Thomas Humphlet. Signed by Worlick Westwood. January 27, 1791 - recorded:Johnson Tabb.

7-9 - **John Smelt** - Account of estate. George Booker, Executor. February, 1788 - Robert Smelt, John Fields, Robert Armistead, Miles King, John Saymour, Doctor Applewhaite, John Perry, David Smelt, William Wager, Col. Westwood, Joseph Smelt, Thomas Ross, Doctor Selden, Doctor Hamm, Robert Wallace, Joseph Cowper, Bartlet Field, Gerrard Seymour, Thomas Wooten, Mrs. Smelt, Adam Gussel, Mrs. Bayley, John Rogers, Mrs. Lively, John Wilson, William Latimer, John Parsons, David Smelt, William Armistead, William Seymour, "Old Abram", Joseph Smelt, Thomas Tabb, Frankey Sewelling, Joseph Meridith, Robert Brough, John Skinner, Miles Smelt. Examiners: Selden Moss, Thomas Allen, John Skinner. January 27, 1791 - recorded: Johnson Tabb.

9-10 - **Robert Wellings** - Appraisement of estate August 25, _____ - Livestock, household items Examiners: Nat. Bell, John Wood, John Allen. January 27, 1791 - recorded:Johnson Tabb.

10 - **John Pool and Jane, his wife / Roe Cooper** December 15, 1790 - Indenture - 19 acres:

Elizabeth City County, Virginia, 1787-1800

beginning at pine stump, on the west side of a branch, on the line between said Pool and Cooper, and running from thence about N10E about nineteen poles to a persimmon tree within eighteen feet of the Cale James Williams line, thence E6N one hundred and sixty poles, to a small marked white gum tree near Whitings new road, thence south to the said Cooper line, thence to the place where it begun. Part of land purchased by said Pool of Doct. Wilson Cary Selden. Wit: Mark Hall, James K. Cowper, Philip Cowper. February 24, 1791 - recorded: Johnson Tabb.

11 - **John Pool / Thomas Bayley** - December 23, 1790 - Indenture for 30 acres: land known as the Thomas Bayley tract where he now lives. Wit: Gerrard Seymour, Joseph Cooper, William Watkins, Miles King, William Armistead. February 24, 1791 - recorded:Johnson Tabb.

11-12 - **Roe Cowper and his wife Jane / John Pool** - December 15, 1790 - Indenture for 9 acres: land purchased by Cowper of George Walker, April 10, 1770: on the north side of a marsh, beginning at an old pine sump, on the west side of a branch, on the line between the said Pool and Cowper land running W6S ninety-seven poles, to the mouth of a creek to high water mark. Thence about a southeast course twenty-eight poles, thence about a northeast course as the bank runs leaving the said Cowper room enough to make a worm fence on high land to continue in a straight line as may be by taking in any small points along the bank to the beginning place. Wit: James K. Cowper, Philip Cowper, Sarah Cowper. February 24, 1791 - recorded:Johnson Tabb.

12 - **Miles King / James Latimer, pilot** - January 28, 1791 - Indenture for 15 acres: part of tract of land lived on by the late William Bennett: beginning at a marked gum and running thence by a line of marked trees along

Elizabeth City County, Virginia, 1787-1800

Servant's line, one hundred and twenty-two poles to Mill Creek, thence up the creek fourteen poles to a stump and stake, thence N41W till it intersects the back line, being the line of a tract of land formerly belonging to Wm. Brough, thence with this line to the beginning. No witnesses. February 24, 1791 - recorded:Johnson Tabb.

13 - **John Parish and his wife / John Harper** February 24, 1791 - Indenture for 3/4 of a lot in town of Hampton: bound on the north by the creek that divides the said town from the land of Wilson Curle, on the east by Hampton River, on the south by the land of Edward Face and on the west by the land of William Thomas. No witnesses. February 24, 1791 - recorded:Johnson Tabb.

13 - **Hampton Warehouse Accounts - Joseph Cooper and John Skinner, Inspectors** - February 24, 1791.

14 - **Rachel Jones and Isaac Redmon of Shelburn, Nova Scotia / Robert Brough** - January 19, 1791 - Sale of slaves: Amy and her two children, Jim and Jack. Morris Jones, Susanna Pastuer Jones, and Penlen a slave mentioned. Wit: Wilson Wallace, John Rogers, William Bryan. February 24, 1791 - recorded:Johnson Tabb.

14-15 - **Rosea Latimer** - Accounting of estate, Geo. Latimer, Admin. July 22, 1790 - James Hannasin, Doctor Applewhaite, William Sandy, William Hunt, William Latimer, John Latimer, Captain James, Thomas Latimer. Wit: Joseph Cooper, Joseph Needham, Arthur Henderson February 24, 1791 - recorded:Johnson Tabb.

15-15a - **Wilson Miles Cary and Sarah his wife / the Rev. James Maddisson, D.D. (Bishop of Virginia)** - March 25, 1791 - Indenture for 161 acres: "Fairfield" and "Lilliput" purchased by

Elizabeth City County, Virginia, 1787-1800

the late Wilson Cary and Wilson Miles Cary from the late John Creek and his wife and the late Curle Tucker and his wife. No witnesses. March 25, 1791 - recorded:Johnson Tabb.

15a-16 - **Rosey Fields / Robert Armistead** - April 28, 1791 - Indenture for 50 acres: Plantation willed by John Nelson to his daughter Hannah Nelson who died and it was taken by her brother John Nelson who gave it to his sister Rosey Fields, widow of John Fields. Bound on the south by land of Edwards Allen, west by Worlick Westwood, north by Robert Armistead. Wit: George Wray, John Perry, Wm. Smith. April 28, 1791 - recorded:Johnson Tabb.

16-18 - **Anthony Armistead of North Carolina / James Burk** - November 27, 1789 - Indenture for 94 acres: lying on Saltford's Creek. Bound north by the land of William Gooch, west by David Jameson, south by Nicholas Bayly, east by Sarah Dixon and Thomas Hatton. William Tucker willed land to Anthony Armistead after the death of his mother Mary Armistead (now Mary Williams). Wit: Benj. Bryan, Thomas Jones, Edward Face, Miles King, Wm. Kirby. April 28, 1791 - recorded:Johnson Tabb.

18-19 - **Rebecca Barron, Miles King, Executors for the late Richard Barron / Wilson Cary Seldon** - March 15, 1791 - Indenture for 100 acres: Plantation on the James River - bound at the River side running north along Henry Jenkins line to the main road, thence along the main road east to Capt. Herbert's line, thence along Capt. Herbert's line south to the James River. No witnesses. April 28, 1791 - recorded: Johnson Tabb.

19-20 - **James Bray Armistead** - Will - August 31, 1790 - Diane Wallace Bayley, wife; Wilson Wallace Bayley, Gill Armistead, son of Captian William Armistead. Slave: Hampton to be freed. Wit: James Goodwin, Samuel Cunningham,

Elizabeth City County, Virginia, 1787-1800

Samuel Burket. April 28, 1791 - recorded: Johnson Tabb.

20-21 - **Ann Wilson** - Will - March 13, 1786 - Elizabeth Been, Martha Been, John Been, James Been, grandchildren; John Skinner, Executor. Slave: Patt. Wit: James Bullock, John Skinner, Mary Bullock. April 28, 1791 - recorded.

21-22 - **Westwood Armistead** - Appraisement of estate - July 17, 1786 - Slaves: George, Peter, Abraham, Jeffery, Charles, Billy, Nanny, Dolly, Rachel, Yellow Lucy, Black Lucy, Grace, Phebe. Also livestock and household items. Appraisers: W.A.T.Parsons, Thos. Allen, Wm. Moore. April 28, 1791 - recorded:Johnson Tabb.

23 - **Robert Willings** - Accounts of estate - **Robert Willings, Exec.** - January 27, 1791 - Johnson Tabb, Miles King, Wm. Seymour, Joseph Nichols, Capt. John Hunter, Capt. Westwood, Mrs. Berry, Mrs. Blaxton. Examiners: Wm. Seymour, John Allen, William Allen. April 26, 1791 - recorded:Johnson Tabb.

24 - **Westwood Armistead Estate** - Court order for division of slaves - Robert Armistead, Westwood Armistead. Slaves: Natt, George, Dolly, Grace, Charles, Peter, Jeffry, Manuel, Rachael, Pheby, Lucy, Billy. Wit: Joseph Needham, William Smith. May 26, 1791 - recorded:Johnson Tabb.

24-25 - **Rachael Jones, Isaac Redmon, Susanna Pasteur Redman / Robert Brough** - May 16, 1791 Sale of slaves: Amy, Jim, Jack. Wit: Minson Crosby, George Minson, William Armistead, Jr., John Perry. June 23, 1791 - recorded:Johnson Tabb.

25-26 - **James Westwood Wallace / Miles King** May 14, 1791 - Indenture for 354 acres: Part of Robert Wallace land beginning at a large stake at the water side running thence south 81 east

Elizabeth City County, Virginia, 1787-1800

149 poles to a large stone in a drain thence up the drain L.31. east 105 poles until it intersects the north 52 1/2 east line of the whole land and thence the different courses and distances to the beginning. Includes a brick windmill. Wit: Joseph Cooper, Wm. King, Richard Dixon, George Cooper, Sheldon Moss, Benjamin Stores. June 23, 1791 - recorded:Johnson Tabb.

26-27 - **William Smith and his wife Elizabeth / Robert Armistead** - June 23, 1791 - Indenture for 18 acres in York County: Tompkins Mill - bound by the dam to the high lands on the south side, then the various courses of the high lands to the county bridge then along the Mill Run to the beginning. William Reed Fathercloth mentioned. June 23, 1791 - recorded:Johnson Tabb.

28 - **Thomas Minson and his wife Ann / Benjamin Stores** - May 14, 1791 - Indenture for 27 acres: bound on the east by the land of Joseph Bushell, on the north by the Main Road, on the west by William Armistead and Samuel Watts, on the south by John Stores. Wit: Charles Jennings, Thomas Latimer, Richard Dixon, Joseph Bushell. June 23, 1791 - recorded.

29 - **Simon Hollier** - Account of estate, Miles King, Admin. - Miles King, Jacob Wray, William Mitchel, Thomas Wootten, Molly, Mr. Brown, Dr. McClurg, Mr. Booker, Johnson Tabb, John Brown, George Latimer, Nathan Yancy, Wm. Wray, Mr. Booker, A. Moore, Thomas Hatten. Slaves: Betty and child, Thaner, Tom, Lucy, Molly, Venus. Examiners: Robert Brough, F. Riddlehurst, John Perry. June 23, 1791 - recorded:Johnson Tabb.

30 - **James B. Armistead** - Appraisement of estate - June 10, 1791 - Slaves: Moses, Hampton. Appraisers: Thomas B. Armistead, Bartlet Fields, John Skinner. June 23, 1791 - recorded:Johnson Tabb.

Elizabeth City County, Virginia, 1787-1800

31-33 - **Thomas Skinner** - Account of estate John Skinner, Executor - Samuel Thomas, Nathan Woody, Mary Moreland, Roby Cokes, William Powell, William Wager, Elizabeth Mason, William Marrow, William Brown, John Wymore, Merrit Westwood, Abia Clay, Sally Skinner, Armiger Webb, Mathew Gouge, James Bray Armistead, Dr. John Brodie, John Armistead John Reid, Mr. Wallace. June 22, 1791 - last entry. Examiners: John Hunter, Miles King, Rob. Brough. June 23, 1791 - recorded:Johnson Tabb.

33-34 - **Thomas Minson, Jr. and Ann his wife / Charles Jennings** - July 11, 1791 - Indenture for 50 acres: beginning at a place in the Jenning's line six poles to the northward of a small sycamore and running thence S76W 54 poles to a stake in a ditch on the side of the road from the house, thence with the ditch and road S4E 147 poles to a road that leads to Fox Hill, thence with the road to Thomas Watts's land, thence with his lands to the said Jennings line, then with the said line to the beginning place. Wit: Miles King, William Price, Hanes Whitfield, Thos. Jones, Wm. Brough. July 28, 1791 - recorded.

34-35 - **Mary Herbert** - November 19, 1790 - Acknowledgement of sale of 50 acres to Thomas Jennings, Jr. Wit: George Hope, Rob. Brough. July 28, 1791 - recorded:Johnson Tabb.

36 - **John Armistead** - Appraisement of estate - March 17, 1791 - Household goods, tools, livestock. Slaves: Sampson, Grisdel, Aron, Molly, China, Sarah and children, Fanny Appraisers: Thomas Allen, James Dixon, Johnson Tabb. July 28, 1791 - recorded:Johnson Tabb.

37 - **John Pauls and his wife Sarah and James Johnson / Worlick Westwood** - August 22, 1791 Indenture for lot in Town of Hampton: bound by George Hope to the west, James Cunningham and Edward Delaney to the south, Worlick Westwood

Elizabeth City County, Virginia, 1787-1800

on the east, and Queen's Street on the north. Wit: John Perry, Jno. Banks, Edward Face, Wm. Watkins, William Hunt, James Burk. September 22, 1791 - recorded:Johnson Tabb.

38 - **James Wood and his wife Margaret / John Harper** - February 26, 1791 - Indenture for a lot in Town of Hampton: bound on the north and west by lands of Edward Face, on the south by John Hicks, on the east by Thomas Pears. Wit: Richard Dixon, George Massenburg, George Thomas. September 22, 1791 - recorded:Johnson Tabb.

39 - **John Harper and his wife Charity / James Wood** - February 26, 1791 - Indenture for land in Town of Hampton: bound on the north by a creek that divides the town from Curles land, on the east by Hampton River, on the south by land of Edward Face, and on the west by land of William Price. Wit: Richard Dixon, George Massenburg, George Thomas. September 22, 1791 - recorded:Johnson Tabb.

40-41 - **James Wood / John Harper** - February 26, 1791 - Indenture for land in Town of Hampton: bound on the north by a creek that divides the town from Curles land, on the east by Hampton River, on the south by land of Edward Face, and on the west by land of William Price. Wit: Richard Dixon, George Massenburg, George Thomas. September 22, 1791 - recorded:Johnson Tabb.

41 - **George Booker / Robert Brough** - July 18, 1791 - Sale of slaves: Mulatto woman named Milly, 26 years old formerly belonging to the estate of Elizabeth Marshall. Wit: John Wray, John Rogers, David Brodie. September 22, 1791 - recorded:Johnson Tabb.

42 - **Job Colton / William Brough** - May 1, 1791 - Sale of slaves and personal estate from Grace Brough, mother of Job Colton's wife Ann.

Elizabeth City County, Virginia, 1787-1800

Robert Brough mentioned. Wit: Edward Ballard, Thomas Jones, John Taner, Warren Hopkins. September 22, 1791 - recorded:Johnson Tabb.

43-45 - **William Cunningham, mariner of Portsmouth and his wife, Elizabeth / George Hope** - July 6, 1791 - Indenture for 1 1/2 acres in the Town of Hampton: land formerly lived on by Samuel Barron Cunningham who purchased it from Roe Cooper on June 24, 1779, who in turned sold it to James Barron and Thomas Wooten August 14, 1783, who sold it to William Cunningham on August 24, 1785. Land is located on the Hampton River. Wit: Worlick Westwood, Peter Ridley, Robert G. Buxton, Warren Hopkin. Acknowledgement of Elizabeth Cunningham. Wit: George Booker, Rob. Brough. September 22, 1791 - recorded:Johnson Tabb.

45-46 - **Blovet Pasteur and his wife Susanah / Robert Buxton** - September 6, 1791 - Indenture for house and land in Town of Hampton: On Queen Street, 34 feet in breadth, in length 112 feet west bound by the line of William Hicks, on the north 40 feet bound by the land of Robert Brough, on the east 112 feet bound by land of Blovet Pasteur. Wit: George Hope, Warren Hopkin, Peter Ridley. September 22, 1791 - recorded: Johnson Tabb.

46-47 - **Francis Ross / Miles King** - March 10, 1791 - Indenture for 50 acres land and slaves: 50 acres on Back River. Slaves: Sarah a wench, Jack a boy, Lettice a girl. Also 12 head of cattle, 10 head of sheep. Wit: John Hunter, Edward Face, Servant Ballard, David Saunders, John Bean. September 22, 1791 - recorded: Johnson Tabb.

48 - **Thomas Wooten** - Will - September 24, 1784 Thomas Wooten, William Wooten, Ann Trigg, Benjamin Wooten, John Wooten, children; Ann Wooten, wife. Land on Harris Creek purchased from William Latimer mentioned. Wit: John

Elizabeth City County, Virginia, 1787-1800

Perry, John Skinner, William King. September 22, 1791 - recorded:unsigned.

49 - **Pascow Herbert and his wife Mary / George Hope** - February 18, 1788 - Acknowledgement of Indenture for 179 acres: land in Sayer [Sawyers?] Swamp by Mary Herbert. Wit: Cary Seldon, Rob Brough. September 23, 1791 - recorded:Johnson Tabb.

50 - **Miles King and his wife Martha / John Moore** - March 4, 1791 - Indenture for 160 acres: formerly owned by Thomas Kerby, deceased. Excepting the graveyard. Bound by lands of William Mallory, John Parsons, deceased, Robert Armistead, and Charles Collier. Wit: Augustine Moore, Jr, William Smith, Richd. Cary, John McKay, Joesph Cooper, Worlick Westwood, Charles Jennings. October 27, 1791 - recorded:Johnson Tabb.

51 - **Henry Jenkins / Pennuel Sands** - March 28, 1791 - Indenture for renting 30 acres: old field grounds of the Henry Jenkins Plantation - 10 or 12 feet from the line between Henry Jenkins land and Doctor Selden's leading westerly from an oak near the line to a pine bush from thence westerly to another pine bush from thence westerly to another. From thence to a little oak near the swamp, thence to the swamp or marsh and then northeasterly along the swamp and side or edge of the woods until it comes within 10 or 12 feet of the line between Jenkins and Seldens land. Wit: Adam Russell, Samuel Burket, Samuel R. Cunningham. October 27, 1791 - recorded:Johnson Tabb.

52 - **John Moore / Miles King** - March 5, 1791 - Indenture of mortgage for ___ acres: Plantation where the late Thomas Kerby lived bound by the lands of William Mallory, William Parsons, and Robert Armistead and the lands of Lackey Collier, deceased. Wit: Richard Cary, Worlick Westwood, Joseph Cooper, Charles Jennings.

Elizabeth City County, Virginia, 1787-1800

October 27, 1791 - recorded:Johnson Tabb.

53 - **William Cary, guardian of Simon Hollier / Ann Hollier** - September 30, 1791 - Indenture for renting farm land of Simon Hollier, orphan of Simon Hollier, deceased. Wit: Miles Cary, Robert Gibbons. October 27, 1791 - recorded: unsigned.

54-55 - **Benjamin Wooten and his wife Mary, of Smithfield / Arthur Henderson** - October 5, 1791 Indenture for 100 acres in Fox Hill - beginning at a pine stump near the marsh by the bridge and running an east course joining Andrew Bully's land until it comes to a marked pine then continues a straight course down to one or two marked pines thence to a creek called Hogshead Quarter thence down northerly to the middle of the said creek a south course to a bridge and thence to the beginning stump. (Sold to Thomas Wooten by William Latimer and his wife Martha, April 5, 1784 and by Thomas Wooten to his son Benjamin.) Wit: Richard Dixon, J. Smith, William Bryan. October 27, 1791 - recorded:unsigned.

55-56 - **Rebecca Dewbre, exec. of will of John Dewbre / James Davis** - June 8, 1791 - Indenture for 20 acres: beginning at an oak adjoining the orphan of William Mholon land from thence to the line of Robert Massenburg's Orphan's and its courses on the said orphan, thence to Samuel Dewbre's line and from thence to Mrs. Dewbre's line. Wit: Gerrard Seymour, Thomas Cobbs, Elizabeth Cobbs, John Bains, David Saunders, Mary Mholon. October 27, 1791 - recorded:Johnson Tabb.

56 - **Worlick Westwood / James Westwood Wallace** - May 16, 1791 - Indenture for lots in Town of Hampton: bound on west by King Street, on the north by land of James Baker, easterly by the land of Mary Chambers, Thomas Garner, John Parish, Benjamin Bryan and Minson Proby,

Elizabeth City County, Virginia, 1787-1800

southerly by land of Richard Barron, deceased. Wit: Augustine Moore, Jr., Jno. Moore, James Barron, William Smith, John Applewhaite, Miles King, William Price, William Kerby. January 26, 1792 - recorded:Johnson Tabb.

57 - **Philip M. Lacklin and his wife Ann / Samuel Barron** - October 15, 1791 - Indenture for lot in Town of Hampton: beginning at the corner of Back Street running along the said street to Hunt's lot thence down the said Hunt's line to the creek thence up the creek to Curle's line thence along Curle's line to the beginning. Wit: Wm. Kerby, David Smelt, Miles Cary, Wm. Hunter. January 26, 1792 - recorded: Johnson Tabb.

58 - **Thomas Paine / Charles Bayley** - August 20, 1791 - Indenture for slave: named Jack. Wit: J. Smith, John A. Wray. January 26, 1792 - recorded:Johnson Tabb.

58-59 - **Wilson Cary Selden / Thomas Hatton** - May 16, 1791 - Release of Deed of Trust for 50 acres: on Saltford's Creek adjoining lands of Miles Cary, Mrs. Sarah Dixon, and James Burke. Deed dated May 18, 1789. Wit: Thomas Jones, John Applewhaite. January 26, 1792 - recorded: Johnson Tabb.

60 - **Mary Courtney Bowery and Grace Elizabeth Bowery** - November 26, 1791 - Receipt of slaves: belonging to estate of William Frazer and recovered from Richard Chapman, guardian of William Frazer. Old Ben, his wife Phobe, their sons Matt, Jesse, and Caleb. Wit: Wm. Brough, Rob Brough, Richd. Hurst. February 23, 1792 - recorded:Johnson Tabb.

61-62 - **Worlick Westwood / Robert Armistead** - June 13, 1791 - Indenture for 50 acres of land: called Herrons, purchased from Henry Allen. Wit: Thos. Allen, Thomas Latimer, William Armistead, Samuel Cunningham, Rich. Hurst.

Elizabeth City County, Virginia, 1787-1800

February 23, 1792 - recorded:Johnson Tabb.

62 - **Elizabeth Parish, John Parish, Jr., William Parish, Mark Parish / Grace Elizabeth Bowery** - December 4, 1791 - Sale of slaves: Sylvia, daughter of Dinah who was bequeathed to Elizabeth Parish by William Parish, deceased. Wit: Henry Dunn, Rob. Brough, Servant Ballard, James Baker. February 23, 1792 - recorded: unsigned.

63 - **John Williams / William Brough** - February 23, 1792 - Sale of slave: man named Lancaster. Wit: Edward Ballard, J. Smith. February 23, 1792 - recorded:Johnson Tabb.

63 - **William Armistead / Robert Armistead** - May 17, 1791 - Gift of three slaves: woman named Hannah and her daughters Moll and Terry. Wit: Miles King, George Wray. February 23, 1792 - recorded:Johnson Tabb.

64 - **Dianna Wallace Bayley** - Will - January 27, 1792 - Slaves: Lucy, Rachel, Tom and Claiborn. Wilson Wallace Bayley, Elizabeth Wallace Bayley, Rachel Mallory, Francis Riddlehurst, Johnson Mallory mentioned. Wit: R. Armistead, David Lively, Rebekah Russell. February 23, 1792 - recorded:Johnson Tabb.

65 - **Samuel Barron / James Barron** - January 21, 1792 - Indenture for 40 acres: North part of Little England tract purchased by the late Commadore James Barron of Benjamin Laport and Captain Joseph Meredith. Land adjoins Miles King. Wit: Joseph Meredith, Wm. Smith, William Guy, William Hunt. February 23, 1792 - recorded:Johnson Tabb.

66-67 - **Thomas Hatton / Wilson Miles Cary** April 17, 1792 - Indenture for 50 acres: beginning at a gum standing in a branch called Slippery Pine falling into Saltford's Creek and joining the lines trees of James Mercer running

Elizabeth City County, Virginia, 1787-1800

thence N5E, 38 poles to a pine corner tree of Anthony Tucker, deceased now belonging to James Burke N25E, 100 poles to a mulberry tree to a corner tree of the land of Thomas Dixon, deceased. Thence S23E, 54 poles to a pine thence south 42 poles to a pine at the head of Slippery Pine Branch corner tree of John Casey's and the said Thomas Dixon's land thence down the branch to the beginning which said land was purchased by Samuel Bains of Willis Skinner and Elizabeth his wife. George Bains mentioned. Wit: Miles King, Thomas Jones, John Perry, George Minson, Robert Elliott, Servant Ballard. April 26, 1792 - recorded:Johnson Tabb.

68 - **Sarah Burt / Thomas Umphlet** - April 25, 1792 - Indenture for 100 acres: not specified by boundaries. Daughters Rebecca and Elizabeth mentioned. Wit: John Minson, Edward Humphlet, James Burke. April 26, 1792 - recorded:Johnson Tabb.

69 - **Joseph Meredith, mariner / Edward Delany** ___ March, 1792 - Release of debt. Wit: John Rogers, Mary Gardnor, Rob Brough. April 26, 1792 - recorded:Johnson Tabb.

70-71 - **William Ap. Thomas Parsons, executor and Mary Parsons, widow of John Parsons / Jacob Wray** - November 11, 1791 - Indenture for 42 acres of land: beginning at a maple stump, standing at the southwest corner of the whole tract and running thence traversing along a line of marked trees north 82 poles to a white oak marked for a corner of this land, thence east 82 poles to an oak sapling marked for a corner, thence south until it intersects the west line of the whole tract by a road, then with this line west to the beginning as surveyed by Richard Dixon. Wit: Worlick Westwood, Catlohill Presson, John Wray, Wm. Davenport, George Wray. June 28, 1792 - recorded:Johnson Tabb.

Elizabeth City County, Virginia, 1787-1800

71-72 - **Thomas Scott of Warwick County / George Hope** - June 28, 1792 - Obligation agreement for debt. Wit: Joseph Meredith, Fras. Ballard, Peter Ridley. June 28, 1792 - recorded:Johnson Tabb.

72-74 - **John Williams and Ann his wife / William Lewis** - June 28, 1792 - Indenture for 144 1/2 acres: beginning at a pine stump on a branch of Harris's Creek running from thence easterly to a pine in a swamp bounded upon Mrs. Williams land, from thence down the swamp to a corner white oak between said Williams and William Latimer and bounding upon said Williams from thence easterly down the said swamp to a corner pine upon the north side of the said swamp, between said Latimer and Thomas Bayley bounding upon Latimer, from thence south eastwardly to a small white gum bounded by said Bayley's land from thence southwestwardly to a corner white oak stump bounded by Samuel Watts and Johnson Mallory's lands from thence northwestwardly to a small white gum upon the south side of the said swamp bounded by the said Mallory's land from thence up the swamp to the large marked pine and from thence westwardly to the mill dam upon a branch of Harris's Creek and bounded upon said Mallory's land and from thence northeastwardly to the pine stump at the beginning. Wit: George Booker, Benjamin Stores, Thomas Lewis. June 28, 1792 - recorded:Johnson Tabb.

75-76 - **Thomas Minson, Jr. and his wife Ann / Joseph Bushell** - February 10, 1792 - Indenture for ___ acres: beginning at a pine near the main road and running thence to a white gum, from thence to a persimmon, from thence to a white gum, from thence to a white gum, from thence to a willow oak, from thence to a sycamore, from thence to a elm in the middle of the swamp as said lines from thence down the middle of the swamp to Thomas Watts's line from thence along the said Watts's line to the main

Elizabeth City County, Virginia, 1787-1800

road from thence along the main road to the beginning pine. Wit: Bauldwin Sheppard, Charles Jennings, Thomas Latimer, Jas. Cooper, Richard Dixon, Mark Hall. June 28, 1792 - recorded: Johnson Tabb.

77-78 - **Thomas Minson, Jr. and his wife Ann / Charles Stores** - June 28, 1792 - Indenture for 3 acres: beginning at a small persimmon tree in the middle of the swamp and running eastwardly up the said swamp to a small persimmon tree bounding upon Joseph Bushell's land from thence southward to a small gum, bounding upon the said Thomas Minson's land, from thence westwardly to a stob drove down within fifteen feet of Frazer Stores, Jr. land bounding upon said Minsons and from thence northwardly to the beginning place, leaving the 15 feet for a road. Wit: Mark Hall, James N. Cooper, Thomas Latimer. June 28, 1792 - recorded:Johnson Tabb.

78-79 - **James B. Armistead** - Accounting of his estate, Diana W. Bayley, Exec. - August 30, 1791 John Applewhaite, Miles King. Slave: Moses, mentioned. Examiners: Thomas B. Armistead, John Skinner, William Landry. June 28, 1792 - recorded:Johnson Tabb.

79-80 - **Moses Armistead** - Accounting of estate - June 1, 1791 - Household items, livestock, Examiners: Joseph Needham, Charles Jennings, George Wray. June 28, 1792 - recorded:Johnson Tabb.

81 - **Thomas Pearse (Parce, Pairce) / Worlick Westwood** - January 16, 1792 - Indenture for lot in Town of Hampton: bounded by lands of John Hicks, John Harper, Edward Face and Hampton River. Wit: William Jennings, Richard Dixon, William Guy, Samuel Bright. July 26, 1792 - recorded:Johnson Tabb.

82 - **Worlick Westwood / Edward Face** - February 22, 1792 - Indenture for lot in Town

Elizabeth City County, Virginia, 1787-1800

of Hampton: bounded by lands of John Hicks, John Harper, Edward Face and Hampton River. Wit: Benjamin Bryan, Thomas Minson, Jno. Banks. July 26, 1792 - recorded:Johnson Tabb.

83 - **Sarah Dixon / Miles King** - November 30, 1791 - Sale of slaves and personal property: Two men, Casear and Pluto. Wm. Kerby, Armistead Whitaker. July 26, 1792 - recorded:Johnson Tabb.

84-85 - **Wilson Curle - Will** - May 25, 1792 - Plantation called Briar Field, Elizabeth Curle, child; Elizabeth Curle, sister; Moss Armistead, William Armistead, Wilson Wallace, lots in Norfolk and Hampton, William Langhorne the Elder, Richard Cary, Maurice Langhorne - mentioned. Wit: George Booker, William Digges, Augustine Moore, Jr. July 26, 1792 - recorded: Johnson Tabb.

86 - **Moses Armistead** - Account of Estate - Miles King, Joseph Selden, John Seymour. Slaves: Tea, Viner, Patty, George, Hannah, Cate, Rachael, Ben, Charles mentioned. Examinters - Miles King, Charles Jennings, Wm. Brough. July 26, 1792 - recorded:Johnson Tabb.

87 - **Ann Wilson** - Appraisement of estate - June 6, 1792 - Slave Patt mentioned. Appraisers: Thos. Minson, John Skinner, Jr., Thomas Humphlet. July 26, 1792 - recorded: Johnson Tabb.

87-88 - **Rev. Mr. William Bland** in Account with Robert Pool - For construction work. Wit: Joseph Cooper, Thomas Fenn, John Lewis. May 24, 1792 - recorded:Johnson Tabb.

88-92 - **John Lowry** - Appraisement of estate - February 7, 1792 - Slaves: Men: Tom, Soney, Frank, Flax, Cato, Charles, Natt, Norfolk, Luke, James, Jacob, Mallica; Boys: Joe, Tuber, Sam, Hammard; Women: Fanar, Molly, Jenny,

Elizabeth City County, Virginia, 1787-1800

Rachel and child, Milly and child, Beck, Murryear, Sarah, Sue; Girls: Sall; Old Nanny, Old Ester - mentioned. Schooner mentioned. Examiners: Joseph Cooper, William Davis, Hugh Moore, Jr. July 26, 1792 - recorded:Johnson Tabb.

93-94 - **Mary Courtney Bowrey, Grace Elizabeth Bowrey, Robert Bowrey against Elizabeth Chapman, Admin. of Richard Chapman, deceased** - October 19, 1791 - High Court of Chancery in Richmond. Slave, Jim; Robert Brough mentioned. Wit: William Brough, John Rogers. September 27, 1792 - recorded:Johnson Tabb.

95-96 - **William Charles Lee / Wilson Cary Selden** - May 25, 1792 - Indenture for 100 acres: Plantation tract on the James River. Bounded eastwardly by lands of Pascow Herbert, westwardly by land of Henry Jenkins, northwardly by the road leading from the said plantation to Hampton. Wit: Benjamin Bryan, Worlick Westwood, Augustine Moore, William King. September 27, 1792 - recorded:Johnson Tabb.

96-97 - **Chaves Elott / Robert Elott (her son) (ELLOTT)** - August 20, 1792 - Indenture for 180 acres: beginning on the mouth of a gut near the mouth of the creek and running up the creek to Capt. Joseph Meredith's line, then up his line to a corner hickory, then up the plantation line to a corner oak, the dividing line between Elizabeth and Ann Mindham, then along a line of marked trees to the marsh and so to the beginning gut. Wit: Robert Armistead, John Latimer, James Turnbull. September 27, 1792 - recorded:Johnson Tabb.

97 - **William Latimer / Euphan Marshall, widow of James Marshall / Samuel Selden** - March 28, 1792 - Indenture: William Latimer after marrying Euphan Marshall, renounces claim to any of her property. Wit: Miles King, Thomas

Elizabeth City County, Virginia, 1787-1800

Latimer, John Rogers, William Hunt. September 27, 1792 - recorded:unsigned.

98 - **Demsey Copeland and his wife Nancy and Betsy Allen, sister of Nancy / Miles King** March 15, 1792 - Indenture for 17 acres: bound by Robert Armistead's, Edward Allen's, and Miles King's land. Wit: Ermin Sandy, William Latimer, James Ballard. September 27, 1792 - recorded:Johnson Tabb.

98 - **Miles King / Thomas Minson, Jr.** - September 27, 1792 - Release of land of 150 acres. Thomas Minson, Jr. in turn has sold parts of land to Charles Jennings, Benjamin Stores. September 27, 1792 - recorded:Johnson Tabb.

99 - **Adam Mercer of Nansemond County / James Burke** - September 1, 1792 - Indenture for 150 acres: beginning at the James River and running west to the line of the Bullocks and running northerly to the land of Bayleys, thence easterly to the land of Col. Cary and Jigetts, and thence along Jigett's line to the James River southerly. Wit: Thomas Jones, Worlick Westwood, Wilson Cary Selden, Miles Cary, David Brodie, Miles King. September 27, 1792 - recorded:Johnson Tabb.

99 - **Miles King / Frasher Stores, Jr.** - April 20, 1792 - Release of land of 50 acres. Frasher Stores, Jr. in turn has sold 8 acres of the land to William Stores. September 27, 1792 - recorded:Johnson Tabb.

100 - **Nathaniel Bell** - Accounting of Estate by Miles King, Sheriff - September 27, 1792 - Debits: James Davis, Doctor Colton, Doctor Applewhaite, Robert Armistead, Miles King, Robert Brough, William Allen, Robert Maney, Robert Holloway, Johnson Tabb, William Sandefur, Thomas Humphlet. Credits: Jane Bell, Robert Maney, Robert Holloway, Miles King, John

Elizabeth City County, Virginia, 1787-1800

Bell, Judith Saunders, Alexander Maney, Thomas Minson, John Skinner, Elizabeth Sandefur, William Sandefur, Robert Sandefur, Col. Westwood, Jno. Hayes, Callohil Minnis, Joseph Smith, James Goodwin. September 27, 1792 - recorded:Johnson Tabb.

101 - **William Sandefur** - Account of Estate with Nath'l Bell - December 14, 1789 - John Allen, Elizabeth Watkins, Aron Barnes, James Lewellen, William Seymour, Richard Crandle, Miles King, John Reid, Col. Langhorn, John Woods, John Dunn, John Wilson, Mr. Nicholson, William Marrow, Mr. Booker, William McGregor, ___Sherington, Hawkins Reid, Natt Bell, Robert Brough, Elizabeth Sandefur, Doctor Haynes mentioned. Examiners: John Hunter, Joseph Needham, Charles Jennings. September 27, 1792 - recorded:Johnson Tabb.

102-105 - **Francis Mallory** - Account of Estate with Miles King for Betsy, Mary, and Charles and sundries for the negroes: Johny the Elder, Johny the Younger, Sam, Abraham, Cate, Ned, Will, Mun, Pegg, Silpha, Lidia, Hannah, Sarah and children, Lucy and children, Judy and children, Rachel and child, Nancy and children, Lee, Manuel, James, Sue, Chelsea, Judea and her children, Euphan Marshall, Francis Minnis, Col. Westwood - mentioned. September 27, 1792 - recorded.

106 - **Job Colton / William Brough** - September 12, 1792 - Sale of slave: Boy named George, part of estate of Robert Brough and inherited by Ann Colton. October 25, 1792 - recorded: Johnson Tabb.

106 - **Thomas Humphlet and Elizabeth his wife / James Daes** - March 31, 1792 - Indenture for 26 acres: half of tract purchased by King Humphlet from Benjamin Powell (except 1/2 acre of ground, the Ancient burying place). Wit: Richard Dixon, William Sandy, William Kerby,

Elizabeth City County, Virginia, 1787-1800

Miles King. October 25, 1792 - recorded:Johnson Tabb.

107 - **Miles King / Thomas Minson, Joseph Bushell, Charles Stores** - October 25, 1792 - Release of deed of trust. October 25, 1792 - recorded:Johnson Tabb.

107 - **Robert Smelt / Miles King** - May 3, 1792 Indenture for slaves and livestock: Man named Colly, girl named Patt and her increase. Wit: William Kerby, Thomas Humphlet. October 25, 1792 - recorded:Johnson Tabb.

108 - **William Gooch - Will** - February 18, 1792 Sarah Gooch, wife; William Gooch, Polly Gooch, Elizabeth Gooch, children. Slaves: Harry, Abby and Hannah mentioned. Wit: Gerrard Seymour, Susannah Dunn. October 25, 1792 - recorded: unsigned.

109 - **William Charles Lee and his wife Catherine / Dr. Anthony Martin of the Town of Portsmouth** - December 25, 1792 - Indenture for 100 acres: binding the land of Capt. Herbert and Jenkins. Land was once property of Dr. Seldum [sic]. Wit: Ralph Pigot, James Newell, Robert Burke, Edmond Warriner. January 24, 1793 - recorded:Johnson Tabb.

109 - **John Rogers / Lucy and child Nancy [Tarrant]** - January 21, 1792 - Emancipation: Lucy and child Nancy (15 months old), who were part of estate of Robert Brough, deceased, father of John Roger's wife. Wit: Samuel Barron, George Hope, George Wray, Jr. January 24, 1793 - recorded:Johnson Tabb.

110 - **Robert Brough Estate / Miles King** - October 27, 1792 - Final accounting and payment Wit: Pascow Herbert, Wilson Miles Cary. January 24, 1793 - recorded:Johnson Tabb.

110 - **Blovett Pasteur and his wife, Susannah /**

Elizabeth City County, Virginia, 1787-1800

Robert Buxton - May 15, 1792 - Acknowledgement of indenture dated September 1, 1791 and witnessed by George Wray and George Hope. January 24, 1793 - recorded:Johnson Tabb.

111-112 - **Robert Armistead, Sr.** - Will - November 12, 1792 - Elizabeth Armistead, daughter; Elizabeth Armistead, mother; Ann Armistead, wife; William Armistead, son mentioned. Slaves: Yellow Bob, Jeffory, Lockey, Wildley, Jack, Big Beck and her child Phillis, Little Fanny, Sal, Milly. Executors: Col. John Cary, Robert Armistead, William Armistead, Sheldon Moses, Johnson Tabb. Wit: Johnson Tabb, Thomas B. Armistead, William Armistead, John Nettles. January 24, 1793 - recorded:unsigned.

112-113 - **John Applewhaite / Miles King** - May 25, 1792 - Indenture for sale of slaves and livestock: Olive, Amey, Daphne and her child. Wit: William Kerby, Servant Ballard. January 24, 1793 - recorded:Johnson Tabb.

113-114 - **Warren Hopkin / George Hope** - January 1, 1793 - Indenture for lot in Town of Hampton: bounded by Wilson Wallace, westerly by William Hunt, northerly by a street commonly known by the name of the Poack Street, and southerly by a branch of the Hampton River. Martha Wallace, Robert Wallace, Thomas Hatton mentioned. Wit: T. Smith, Jno. Banks, Servant Ballard. January 24, 1793 - recorded:Johnson Tabb.

114 - **Anne Skinner** - Will - January 4, 1793 Thomas Skinner and Rosey Skinner, children mentioned. Wit: Mark Hall, John Been. January 24, 1793 - recorded:unsigned.

115-116 - **James Marshall** - Appraisement of April 14, 1792 - Household goods, livestock, and slaves: Jacob, Roger, Harry, Samuel, Rose, Patty, Lea, Kitty, Viner, Minon, Rachel. Examiners: Joseph Cooper, Charles Jennings,

Elizabeth City County, Virginia, 1787-1800

Joseph Needham. January 24, 1793 - recorded: Johnson Tabb.

116-117 - **Francis Mallory** - Appraisement of slaves - December 31, 1788 - Sue, Lucy and her children Davy and Bob, Lewis, Bill, Ben, Sam Berry, Sam, Johnny, Manuel, Jack, Abraham, Johnny, Ned, Mun, Deb, Lidia and her children James and Peter; Judia, Rachael and her child James; Tom, Billy, Sarah and her children Silpha, Mary, Betty, Silvy; Hanah, Nancy and her child Chelcey, Matt, Nelly and her children Jolly, Hannaball, Rose; Old Hannah and her child Peggy. Mary Mallory, George Wray, Elizabeth Mallory, Charles Mallory, Francis Mallory, Dianna Wray mentioned. Wit: John Cary, Sheldon Moses, William Moore. March 25, 1793 - recorded:Johnson Tabb.

118 - **Edward Cutiller and Mary his wife / John Kerby** - July 2, 1791 - Indenture for 16 acres: bounded by the lands of William Mallory on the south side of the road leading towards the free school on Back River and on the edge of the lands of George Wythe the said 16 acres being formerly a part of the tract of the said George Wythe and was given in exchange by Margaret Wythe the mother of George Wythe for 16 and 2/3 acres of land lying and being upon the old Poquoson River and bounded by the lands of Thomas Wythe on three sides and on the southside by John George. Hannah Francis mentioned. Wit: Starkey Robinson, Jr., Henry Howard, B. Dedman. (Note: signed by Abraham Cutiller) - April 25, 1793 - recorded:Johnson Tabb.

119 - **Frazier Stores** - Will - March 15, 1790 Martha Marshall, housekeeper; Jane Ross, daughter; Elizabeth Frazier Randle, Ann Randle, John Randle, James Randle, grandchildren; John Randle, son-in-law - mentioned. Slave Abraham to be freed upon death of Martha Marshall. Wit: Mark Hall, Andrew Bully, Baldwin Morris.

Elizabeth City County, Virginia, 1787-1800

April 25, 1793 - recorded:Johnson Tabb.

120 - **Mary Smith** - Will - November 9, 1792
Richard H. Smith, Hannah Simpson, Mary Smith, Fanny Smith, Elizabeth Smith, William Smith - children. Land: bound by Mr. Rowland on the west, down to the River. A second parcel of 40 acres headed on the North by Col. Cary's land. Wit: Gerrard Seymour, Johnson Ross, Samuel Rowland. April 25, 1793 - recorded:Johnson Tabb.

121 - **Samuel Cunningham / William Cunningham**
April 23, 1793 - Indenture for 25 acres to rent: part of Eaton Free School land. Wit: Gerrard Seymour, Thomas Hatten, Jos. Selden, John Banks. April 25, 1793 - recorded:Johnson Tabb.

121-122 - **Samuel Cunningham / James Cunningham**
April 23, 1793 - Indenture for 25 acres to rent: part of Eaton Free School land. Wit: Gerrard Seymour, Thomas Hatten, Jos. Selden, John Banks. April 25, 1793 - recorded:Johnson Tabb.

122 - **Samuel Watts, Sr. and Jane his wife / James Naylon Cooper, grandson** - April 10, 1793 Indenture for 50 acres: adjoining northwardly the land of Robert Wallace, dec'd. Wit: Wilson Cary Selden, Andrew Bully, Samuel Watts, Jr. April 25, 1793 - recorded:Johnson Tabb.

123 - **Worlick Westwood / Robert Haughton of Warwick County** - October 1, 1792 - Indenture for 65 acres: Remainder of Oppossum Hall, after deducting Robert Maney's 25 acres bounded easterly and northerly on the land of Robert Maney, southerly on the land of John Wood, westerly on the land of Hudson Allen, dec'd. also northerly on the land of Samuel Thomas. Wit: John A. Wray, Michl. King, M. Moore, W.A.T.Parsons. April 25, 1793 - recorded: Johnson Tabb.

Elizabeth City County, Virginia, 1787-1800

123 - **William Latimer, Sr. / George Latimer, son** - April 10, 1792 - Indenture for 25 acres: on Fox Hill adjoining lines of the lands of Arthur Henderson and the land of Thomas Bayley, dec'd. Wit: Benjamin Bryan, George Booker, Joseph Cooper. April 25, 1793 - recorded: Johnson Tabb.

124 - **Phebey Hurst / Samuel Rowland** - April 10, 1793 - Indenture for 25 acres to rent. Wit: Benj. Bryan, Richard Rowland, Richard H. Smith. April 25, 1793 - recorded:Johnson Tabb.

124 - **Letter from Philip Parcell in London giving Joseph Selden power of attorney** to sell property - November 9, 1792 - Property: Brig Two Brothers and sloop Chancis. Miles King, George Booker, Jacob Wray, Rough Couper mentioned. April 25, 1793 - recorded:Johnson Tabb.

125 - **Augustine Moore / Augustine Moore the Younger** - October 10, 1792 - Indenture for the "Old House" and 25 acres: bound on the east by Mrs. Mary Tabb, on the west and north by Augustine Moore, Sr., and on the south by Col. John Cary. Wit: William Seymour, Michael King, William Moore. April 25, 1793 - recorded: Johnson Tabb.

126 - **Mary Powell** - Will - June 20, 1792 Francis Riddlehurst, uncle; Elizabeth Riddlehurst, aunt; Catherine Armistead, cousin; Mary Carlton, Jr., cousin; Pricilla Mitchell, cousin; John Perry, friend - mentioned Slaves: Lender and her children, Tim, Jeffrey, Joe to be set free at death of aunt and uncle. Wit: Anne Jones, John Perry. June 25, 1793 - recorded:Johnson Tabb.

127 - **George Booker, William Moore, David Brodie / Governor of Virginia** - April 25, 1793 Obligation bond for office of Sheriff for George Booker. Recorded:Johnson Tabb.

Elizabeth City County, Virginia, 1787-1800

128 - **George Booker, William Moore, David Brodie / Treasurer of Virginia** - April 25, 1793 Obligation bond for office of Sheriff for George Booker. Recorded:Johnson Tabb.

128-129 - **Joseph Cooper / John Cooper, son** September 6, 1793 - Indenture for 62 1/2 acres: half of plantation adjoining Mary Latimer's land. Wit: Thomas Allen, William Sandy, Thomas B. Armistead. September 26, 1793 - recorded: Johnson Tabb.

130 - **John Banks / John Perry** - May 14, 1792 - Sale of slave named Sam. Wit: Edward Face, William Smith. September 26, 1793 - recorded: Johnson Tabb.

130-131 - **John Harper, and Charity his wife / Cesar Tarrant** - April 15, 1793 - Indenture for land in Town of Hampton: Bound on the north and west by Edward Face, on the south by John Hicks, and on the east by Thomas Pearse. Land was purchased by John Harper of James Wood and Margaret his wife. Wit: Miles King, George Massenburg, Thomas Lewis. September 26, 1793 - recorded:Johnson Tabb.

131-132 - **Thomas Minson and Ann his wife / Ann Boutwell** - September 18, 1793 - Indenture for 6 acres: Adjoining Mr. Charles Jennings and beginning at a small sapling gum as a corner tree near an old road about a south course to the Main Road, thence about a west course along the said Main Road 18 poles to a causeway that did lead down to Cowper's old house, from thence along the said road about a north course to a young sapling pine as a corner tree near the said road from thence an east course to a sapling gum at the beginning place. Wit: Joseph Cooper, James N. Cooper, William Armistead, Charles M. Collier. September 26, 1793 - recorded:Johnson Tabb.

132-133 - **James Baker / Miles King** -

Elizabeth City County, Virginia, 1787-1800

February 22, 1793 - Indenture for land: willed to Baker by his father. Adjoining the land of William Armistead, Miles King, and Samuel Selden. Wit: Miles Cary, William Allen, John Harper. September 26, 1793 - recorded:Johnson Tabb.

133-134 - **Jane Barron / Miles King** - March 15, 1793 - Indenture for land: Little England and wood tract sold by King to Samuel and James Barron. Wit: James Turnbull, Mary Turnbull, Edward Mallory. September 26, 1792 - loaged for further proof.

134 - **John Weymouth** - Will - January 4, 1793 Anne Weymouth, wife; John Wilson, Jr. mentioned. Wit: John Drewry, William Allen, William Drewry. September 26, 1793 - recorded: Johnson Tabb.

134-135 - **Frazer Stores** - Appraisement of Estate - Personal and household goods, livestock. Slaves: Phill, Will, Nanney, Lucey, Natt, Billy, Phill, Jr., Joe, Sam. Appraisers: Joseph Cooper, Thomas Watts, James N. Cooper. September 26, 1793 - recorded:Johnson Tabb.

136 - **William Lewis** - Will - November 26, 1793 142 acres to son William. Lands in lower Fox Hill to be sold for debts. Daughters Jane, Sarah, Elizabeth and Ann mentioned. Executors: Mark Hall, William Latimer. Wit: Mark Hall, Robert Brown, Richard Routon. September 26, 1793 - recorded:Johnson Tabb.

137 - **John Bennett / John Jennings** - May 21, 1793 - Indenture for 1/7th part of 25 acres John Bennett inherited. Wit: Miles King, James Ba___, Joseph Meredith. December 26, 1793 - recorded:Johnson Tabb.

138 - **Worlick Westwood and Hannah his wife / George Wray** - January 2, 1794 - Indenture for 80-100 acres: bound on the south and west by

Elizabeth City County, Virginia, 1787-1800

William Armistead, Sr., on the North by Jacob Wray and Johnson Tabb, on the east by Jacob Wray. Wit: John Wray, Jno. Banks, Jas. Banks, John Banks, John Harper, Edward Face. February 27, 1794 - recorded:Johnson Tabb.

139 - **Joseph Prentis, Richard Cary, Miles King, Worlick Westwood as Commissioners appointed by the General Assembly for public lands / Roe Cowper** - Auction sale of Little Scotland on the east side of the Hampton River containing 60 acres and formerly the property of James Belfour. W. Davenport as to Jos. Prentis; Henry Hirst as to Jos. Prentis; Robert Presson as to J. Prentis; Charles Bayley, Richard Cary, Miles King, Worlich Westwood. February 27, 1794 - recorded:M. Moore.

140 - **Mark Hall** - Will - April 18, 1793 - Slave, Nan. Wife and children not mentioned by name. Wit: Thomas Minson, Jr., William Kerby, Rebecah Russel, David Hall. February 27, 1794 - recorded:unsigned.

141 - **Frazer Stores** - Division of Estate by Court Order - March 28, 1794 - John Randle, Elizabeth Frazer, Ann Randle, James Randle, John Bennett, George Walker, Jane Ross mentioned. Slaves - Phill, Lucey, Natt, Billy, Nanny, Joe, Sam, Will. Examiners: Joseph Cooper, Thomas Watts, James N. Cooper. March 27, 1794 - recorded:Johnson Tabb.

141-142 - **Frazer Stores** - Accounting of Estate August 22, 1793 - John Randle, Mr. Skyrin, Mr. King, Col. Westwood, Mr. Perry, Mr. Jones, Mr. Booker, B. Smith, Mr. Tabb. Examiners: Joseph Cooper, Thomas Watts, James N. Cooper. March 27, 1794 - recorded:Johnson Tabb.

142 - August 23, 1793 - Decreetal Order for division of slaves. John Stith Westwood, Judith Westwood, William King, Mary King, James Bayley, Walter Bayley mentioned. Slaves -

Elizabeth City County, Virginia, 1787-1800

Lydia, Mary, Fanny, Rose, Billy, Caroline. Subscribers: Thomas B. Armistead, Bartlet Field, Joseph Needham. March 27, 1794 - recorded:Johnson Tabb.

143-144 - **William Brough / James Drew McCan of Henrico County** - April 1, 1794 - Indenture for 400 acres: plantation on the east side of the Hampton River bound southwardly by the Glebe land, northwardly by the land of John Robinson, deceased, eastwardly by the land of David Mead. Wit: Benjamin Bryan, James Smith, Minson Proby, George Hope, Cary Selden. April 24, 1794 - recorded:Johnson Tabb.

144 - **Capt. John Harris** - settlement of estate - April 21, 1794 - Executors: William Plume, William Brough. Sarah McCan mentioned. Wit: James Smith, Minson Proby, Benjamin Bryan, George Hope. April 24, 1794 - recorded:Johnson Tabb.

145-146 - **Wilson Cary Selden / John Page of Matthews County** - October 17, 1793 - Indenture for 1000 acres: The Buckroe Tract - beginning westwardly at a corner hickory from the lands of Walker northwardly by the lands of Shepard and Rachael Mallory, eastwardly by the lands of Samuel Watts down to Long Creek Bridge and up the said creek to the beach. Wit: Benjamin Bryan, Miles Cary, David Meade, Cary Selden. (Note: The Selden family may cut firewood from land). April 24, 1794 - recorded:Johnson Tabb.

147-148 - **Minson Proby, carpenter / William Armistead, ship carpenter** - November 26, 1793 Indenture for house in Town of Hampton: bounded on the north by Warren Hopkins, on the south by Mrs. Jones, on the east by Queen Street, on the west by rest of Minson Proby lot. Minson Proby got the land from Charles Hundley who inherited it from his brother Robert Hundley who in turn had inherited it from his father Robert Hundley. Wit: George Hope, John Barraclough,

Elizabeth City County, Virginia, 1787-1800

George Hope, Jr. Mary Proby - signature
April 24, 1794 - recorded:Johnson Tabb.

148-149 - **Charles Jennings / Thomas Watts**
January 1, 1794 - Indenture for 49 1/2 acres: beginning at a Pine near the edge of the marsh on Harris's Creek and running from thence S50E, 98 1/4 poles by a sycamore stump near the grave yard to between two pines marked as side lines, thence S10 E, 112 poles by a pine in the edge of the Old Field to a small white gum a corner between the said Jennings, Sheppard and Thomas Watts thence along said Watts line S6.6E, 34 1/2 poles to a stake a corner between the said Jennings, Watts & Thomas Minson, Jr., thence along said Minson's line N8W, 43 poles to a white gum North 18 poles to a pine N20W, 26 poles to a pine N30 1/2W 26 poles to a pine N30 1/2W 127 to Harris's Creek thence along the said creek the several courses thereof 53 poles thence S67E, 10 poles to the beginning corner pine near the edge of the marsh. Wit: John Cooper, Thomas Jennings, William Jennings. April 24, 1794 - recorded:Johnson Tabb.

150 - **William Armistead / Sarah Armistead**
July __, 1793 - Sale of slaves: Jenny, Lydia, Rachael, boy called America. Wit: Richard Cary, Miles Cary. April 24, 1794 - recorded:Johnson Tabb.

150 - **William Armistead / Euphan Armistead**
October 3, 1793 - Sale of slave: Rose. Wit: Richard Cary, Miles Cary. April 24, 1794 - recorded:Johnson Tabb.

151 - **William Armistead/Mary Armistead**
October 3, 1793 - Sale of slaves: Hester and child, Charlotte, Emmanuel. Wit: Richard Cary, Miles Cary. April 24, 1794 - recorded:Johnson Tabb.

152-153 - **Robert Sandefer Reade of Halifax, Virginia, Attorney for Anne Haynes / Thomas**

Elizabeth City County, Virginia, 1787-1800

Robinson of Charles and York County - March 20, 1794 - Indenture for two hundred acres: in Elizabeth City County. Wit: H. Reade, George Purdie, Jr., Everd. Robinson, Robert Sandefer, John Kerby. Note: Robert Sandefer Reade is Mary Haynes's son. Wit: T. Hall, John Dunkley, George Hudson. April 24, 1794 - recorded: Johnson Tabb.

154 - **Thomas Jennings** - Will - July 20, 1791 Elizabeth Jennings, wife; Charles Jennings, John Jennings, William Jennings, Thomas Jennings, sons; Jean Robinson, daughter; Thomas Robinson, Henry Robinson, grandchildren; Susanah Rudd, daughter mentioned. Slaves: Ned, Peter, Sam, Will, Hanah, Sarah, Moll, Jack Wit: John Parish, William Dobbins, Saley Parish. July 24, 1794 - recorded:unsigned.

155 - **Martha Ross** - Will - September 12, 1787 Elizabeth Ross, Euphan Ross, Deannah Ross, daughters; Cheely Ross, Johnson Mallory Ross, sons; George Booker, Johnson Tabb mentioned. Slaves: Will, Mary, Neptune. Wit: Johnson Tabb, William Ap. Thomas Parsons. July 24, 1794 - recorded:unsigned.

155-157 - **Miles King, John Rogers, Charles Jennings (disposing of by auction by Act of Assembly at Richmond) / John Hutchings, mariner** July 2, 1794 - Indenture for land of Michael Counsel, dec'd.: in Town of Southampton: beginning at the east side of a brick house, turning north the line of Francis Riddlehurst thence west to an old chimney, thence south to the south corner of the same chimney thence west to the Colledge Land thence south to the water course thence east as far as the east corner of the brick house. Michael Counsel bought land of Roe Cowper and his wife Mary. Michael Counsel died without heir. Wit: John Bright, Charles Jones, William Allen, William Brough, Minson Proby. July 24, 1794 - recorded: Johnson Tabb.

Elizabeth City County, Virginia, 1787-1800

157 - **John Williams, Administrator of William Lewis, deceased / Thomas Lewis** - July 24, 1794 Indenture for 12 acres: bound on the north by Whitehall Creek, on the south by John Clark, on the east by the late Matthew Lewis, on the west by Andrew Bully. July 24, 1794 - recorded: Johnson Tabb.

158 - **John Williams, Administrator of William Lewis, deceased / John Clark** - July 24, 1794 Indenture for 25 acres: adjoining land of Thomas Bully, Robert Poole, Thomas Lewis and the late Matthew Lewis. July 24, 1794 - recorded:Johnson Tabb.

159-160 - **John Bushell, Jr. and Elizabeth his wife / Thomas Cain** - December 11, 1793 - Indenture for 10 acres: beginning at a gum a mark tree between Thomas Bully and Thomas Bayle's, deceased, and thence a south course along the said line to a small gum near the corner and from thence east course to a gum near the road and from thence to the middle of the cove, from thence along said cove to the said Thomas Bully's land a north course and from thence along the said Bulley's land a west course to the beginning place. Property was bought by John Bushell of John Skinner in April of 1788. Wit: Joseph Cooper, Robert Brown, George Cooper. July 24, 1794 - recorded: Johnson Tabb.

160 - **John Ashton Wray, George Wray, George Booker / Henry Lee, Governor of Virginia** July 24, 1794 - Obligation bond for John Ashton Wray as surveyor of Elizabeth City County. July 24, 1794 - recorded:Johnson Tabb.

161-162 - **Seth Foster as guardian of John Stark King, heir of John King / Frederick Williams and James Boyce, Executors of the last will of William Armistead Bailey, deceased, of Norfolk** June 7, 1794 - Indenture for two lotts in Town of Hampton: lying on Kings Street bound on the

Elizabeth City County, Virginia, 1787-1800

south by the lot of John Perry, on the west by the colledge lot, and on the north by a small alley. Widow Ann mentioned. Wit: John Drewery, Charles Jones, William Allen, Joseph Cooper. Jr. July 24, 1794 - recorded:Johnson Tabb.

162-163 - **Seth Foster and Anne his wife / Miles King** - June 2, 1794 - Indenture for lots in Town of Hampton. John King, William Armistead Bailey mentioned. Wit: Cary Selden, George Booker, Robert Elliott, George Hope. July 24, 1794 - recorded:Johnson Tabb.

164-165 - **Miles King and Martha his wife / Angelique Henretta Louslow Herren Carbier** July 24, 1794 - Indenture for 354 acres called Erroll: tract formerly belonging to the late Robert Wallace and inherited by James Westwood Wallace: Beginning at a stone at the waterside near the center of the saw pit and running easterly to a large corner stone in a drain thence running southerly along the drain to Naylor's line thence along the line to Watt's land to the main road thence along the main road westerly until it meets Baker's line thence along Baker's line until it comes to the dividing line of _____ orphan's thence along said line until it comes to Joseph Needham's line thence along his line to the River thence along the river to the beginning place. Acknowledgement that Martha agrees with sale of land. Wit: Worlick Westwood, George Wray. July 24, 1794 - recorded:Johnson Tabb.

166 - **James Parsons - Letter of Expatriation** June 11, 1794 - Relinquishes his citizenship of the Commonwealth of Virginia. Wit: John Bright, William Smith, William Guy. Thomas Jones, Notary Public. July 24, 1794 - recorded: Johnson Tabb.

167-168 - **Deana Wallace Bailey** - appraisement of estate - January 28, 1792 - Household goods. Slaves: Rachael, Lucy, Tom May, Clabourne.

Elizabeth City County, Virginia, 1787-1800

Appraisers: Thomas B. Armistead, John Skinner, William Sandy. July 24, 1794 - recorded: Johnson Tabb.

168 - **Paul Carbier** - appraisement of estate - March 27, 1794 - Household goods. Slaves: Adronus, Antoine, Joseph, Louisia, Anna, Casoline, Jane. Appraisers: William Latimer, Joseph Cooper, William Latimer, Jr., William King, Jr. July 24, 1794 - recorded:Johnson Tabb.

169 - **Robert Armistead / Joseph Meredith** June 13, 1794 - Indenture for house and lott in Hampton. Wit: John Perry, John Banks, James Smith. September 25, 1794- recorded:Johnson Tabb.

170 - **Miles King and his wife Martha / James Borrowdale** - September 25, 1794 - Indenture for lot and house in Hampton: bound on the north by the lot of William C___, on the South by the lot of the late John Jones, on the east by the River and on the west by King Street. Wit: John Perry, William Kirby, John Barraclough. September 25, 1794 - recorded:Johnson Tabb.

171 - **Mary Curle, widow of William Roscow Wilson Curle / Charles Jennings** - February 1, 1794 - Indenture for renting farm: bound northerly by the Plantation belonging to Brights Estate, easterly by the Hampton Creek being a branch of the River, southerly by a marsh that runs through the whole plantation and westerly by the public road. Wit: Joseph Cooper, James N. Cooper, Samuel Watts, Jr., William Pierce, Jno. Steeth Westwood. September 25, 1794 - recorded:Johnson Tabb.

172 - **Mary Latimer** - Will - April 8, 1794 - John Latimer, George Latimer, Thomas Latimer, sons; Jane Watts, daughter; Thomas Watts, John Cooper mentioned. Wit: Joseph Cooper, Joseph Cooper, Jr., George Latimer. September 25, 1794

Elizabeth City County, Virginia 1787-1800

- recorded:Johnson Tabb.

173-174 - **Joseph Meredith and his wife Elizabeth / Robert Armistead** - June 13, 1794 Indenture for lots in the Town of Southampton: bound southward on Queen Street, westward by lot of David Davis, northward by the lot of William and Mary Colledge, eastward by King's Street. Wit: John Perry, John Banks, James Smith. September 25, 1794 - recorded:Johnson Tabb.

175-176 - **Worlick Westwood / Joanna Finnie, widow of Prince George County** - July 1, 1794 Indenture for 230 acres - plantation Good Wood, lying in Sawyer's Swamp and adjoining lands of George Wray, William Armistead, John Tabb, Robert Armistead, deceased, and Miles King. Wit: Benjamin Bryan, James Borrowdale, David Speers, William Smith. September 25, 1794 - recorded:Johnson Tabb.

176-177 - **Jane Watts** - Sale of slaves - September 22, 1794 - John Cooper, Susanna Cooper, William Cooper, Euphan Naylor Russell, Betsy Buxton, Sally Buxton. Slaves: Change, Mall, Whitty. Wit: Joseph Cooper, James N. Cooper, Joseph Cooper, Jr. September 25, 1794 - recorded:Johnson Tabb.

177 - **Charles Bayley** - Will - March 8, 1794 Frances Bayley, wife; William Bayley, Charles Bayley, Thomas Bayley, sons mentioned. Wit: Pascow Herbert, Samuel Healy, James Cunningham, Sedwell Armistead. September 25, 1794 - recorded:unsigned.

178-179 - **James Borrowdale / Miles King** September 25, 1794 - Indenture for lot and house in Hampton that Borrowdale still owed a debt on to Miles King. September 25, 1794 - recorded:Johnson Tabb.

179-181 - **Robert Poole, Sr. and Mary his wife**

Elizabeth City County, Virginia 1787-1800

of Norfolk County / James Latimer
September 10, 1794 - Indenture for 350 acres: in Foxhill, lying on the Bay shore near the mouth of the Back river except for the graveyard. Wit: Miles King, John Bright, George Minson, Henry Skyrin. January 22, 1795 - recorded:Merritt Moore.

182 - **William and Mary College Masters and President / Robert Armistead** - February 20, 1795 - Indenture for 1/2 acre in Town of Hampton: bound by King Street on the east, lot of Robert Armistead on the south, the Court House Lane and the lot of Richard Dixon. James Madison, Pres., Robert Andrews, Math Prof., S. G. Tucker, Prof. of Law and Police, John Bracken, Hum. Prof., James Henderson II, Hum. Prof. February 26, 1795 - recorded: Merritt Moore.

183 - **William King, Jr. / Hannah King, his mother** - November 27, 1794 - Gift of land: one half of his land and house on the James River and slaves Jack, Nancy and Violet. William King mentioned. Wit: Henry Jenkins, Rosea Jenkins. January 22, 1795 - recorded:Merritt Moore.

183-184 - **William Manice / Grace Elizabeth Bowery** - November 10, 1794 - Gift of slaves: Jesse, Caleb, and Sylvia. Wit: Job Colten, Rob Brough, Edward Delany, John Rogers.
February 26, 1795 - recorded:Merritt Moore.

184-185 - **John James Ward of England/Mary Courtney Bowery, his future wife / William and Robert Brough** - January 4, 1795 - Indenture tripartite: possessions of Mary Courtney Bowery, which includes a town lot and slaves Ben and Phoebe will belong to her. Wit: Henry Skyrin, John Finney, William Guy, J. Dubonde, David Hicks. February 25, 1795 - recorded: Merritt Moore.

Elizabeth City County, Virginia 1787-1800

185-187 - **Robert Brough and Elizabeth his wife of Norfolk County / Mary Courtney Bowery** December 29, 1794 - Indenture for lot in Town of Hampton: bound on the east by North Street, on the west by land of the estate of Cornelius Thomas and James Manson, deceased, on the north by a lot formerly owned by John Banks, deceased and on the South by the lot belonging to John Rogers, Blovet Pasteur, John Jennings, and the estate of Robert Buxton, deceased. William Proby, William Hicks, Anne Armistead mentioned. Wit: Jno. Finney, William Broughe, William Guy, J. Dubond, David Hicks, William Pierce, J. Sans. William Newsome, Edward Archer, John Shields, Thomas Brent, Justices of the Peace of Norfolk acknowledge signature of Elizabeth Broughe. February 25, 1795 - recorded:Merritt Moore.

188 - **Wilson C. Wallace / William Latimer, Sr.** January 1, 1795 - Indenture for 100 acres belonging to the late Martha Wallace: bound on the land of Dunn's orphan, William Latimer and the land of Robert Wallace and on the Back River on the north. Wit: John Bright. February 26, 1795 - recorded:Merritt Moore.

189-190 - **Frederick Williams and James Boyce, executors for William Armistead Bayley / Miles King** - July 1, 1794 - Indenture for land which Cary Selden still owed money to William Armistead Bayley. Two lots in Town of Hampton. Wit: James Banks, Francis Ballard, Henry Skyrene, Thomas Wylde, George Booker, David Brodie. January 22, 1795 - recorded:Merritt Moore.

190-191 - **William Armistead, Jr. / George Hope** June 26, 1795 - Obligation bond for George Hope as administrator of estate of James Dixon and for managing the estate of Moseley Armistead for his infant children William Armistead and Anthony Armistead. Wit: Benjamin Bryan, Pascow Herbert, John Rogers, Thomas Jones. June 26,

Elizabeth City County, Virginia 1787-1800

1795 - recorded:Merritt Moore.

191-194 - **William Cary and Sarah his wife of Warwick County and Mary Beverly Smallwood of Norfolk County / George Hope** - June 12, 1795 Indenture for plantation that had been willed to Sarah Cary and Mary Beverly Smallwood by their late father Josiah Massenburg. Wit: Richard Cary, Miles Cary, William Dudley, Catherine Massenburg. Verification of the willingness of Sarah Cary to sell the land. Wit: William Digges, William Dudley. June 26, 1795 - recorded:Merritt Moore.

194-196 - **Wilson Cary Selden and his wife Nelly of Loudon County / Joseph Meredith** - May 30, 1795 - Indenture for tenaments and lots of land in the Town of Hampton: one on North Street and where Wilson Miles Cary formerly lived on purchased from William Minson and his wife Mary, one lying on the west side of North Street which Wilson Miles Cary purchased of William Mitchell, and one on North Street adjoining lot 49 purchased by Wilson Miles Cary of William Skinner. One lot of land on the east side of Wine Street purchased of James Bullock and Mary his wife. Wit: John A. Wray, Benjamin Bryan, William Brough, John Rogers, John Cooper, David Brodie. September 24, 1795 - recorded:M. Moore.

197 - **Anthony F. Dixon and his wife Anne of Charles City County / Richard Backhouse** July 16, 1795 - Indenture for 250 acres: Bound south and southwest by land of W.M. Cary, west by land of William Diggs, on the northwest by lands of William Gooch and on the north by lands formerly of Anthony Hawkins and the Mill Marsh, on the east by Saltford's Creek. Wit: John Moore, Thomas Jones, William Smith. September 24, 1795 - recorded:Merritt Moore.

198-200 - **James Borrowdale and his wife Anne Rosetta / Thomas Jones, Jr.** - May 1, 1795 -

Elizabeth City County, Virginia 1787-1800

Indenture for sale of land to offset purchase of boat <u>Charles</u>. Land is a lot in town of Hampton purchased by Borrowdale of Miles King. Wit: William Kerby, Augustine Moore, Jr., Thomas Kerby. William A.T. Parsons, and Michael King acknowledge Anne Borrowdale's willingness to contract. September 24, 1795 - recorded: Merritt Moore.

201-202 - **Samuel Barron and Elizabeth his wife, James Barron and Elizabeth Mosley his wife / George Hope** - August 28, 1795 - Indenture for lot in Southampton: beginning at a stake on the side of a cove which lies back of Francis Ballards and Henry Sinclairs lots, thence westerly along a lot formerly Boyds to a lot called Oswald's formerly Irvin's thence along the said lot to the Hampton River measuring along the river to Francis Ballards. Thus the Hampton River is on the south, the lots of Oswalds and Irvins on the west, Queen Street on the north and former lots of John Mitchell, now Francis Ballard on the east. William Westwood, Mary Armistead, Robert Armistead, Abraham Mitchell, Samuel Allyne mentioned. Wit: George Wray, George Booker, John Applewhaite, Henry Jenkins. September 24, 1795 - recorded:Merritt Moore.

202-203 - **Thomas Latimer and Euphan his wife / George Hope** - January 16, 1795 - Indenture for 25 acres: on Scones dam bound on the south by Warwick Road, on the east by Thomas Minson, on the north by George Hope, on the West by Mr. Manson. Wit: George Cooper, Thomas Minson, Jr., Ba. Blacke, Joseph Cooper, Jr. September 24, 1795 - recorded:Merritt Moore.

204-205 - **Edward Cowper / George Hope** - August 28, 1795 - Indenture for one moiety of a lot in Town of Southampton: lying on North Street bound by the east, west, north and south by the land of George Hope. Land formerly belonged to Bethia Allen. Wit: Edward Face,

Elizabeth City County, Virginia 1787-1800

Michael King, Charles Jennings. September 24, 1795 - recorded:Merritt Moore.

205-206 - **Rachael Mallory, widow of Edward Mallory / Johnson Mallory, her son** - August 1, 1795 - Indenture for 250 acres: tract of land where Edward Mallory formerly lived. Wit: William King, Jr., James Waller Williams, Thomas Cain, James G. Mallory. September 24, 1795 - recorded:Merritt Moore.

206-207 - **Thomas Wellings and Elizabeth, his wife / John Wilson** - October 22, 1795 - Indenture for 38 acres devised by Mary Wood to Elizabeth: beginning at a corner willow oak between this land and the lands of Mrs. Dewbry and Michael King and running along King's line N9.45E 24 1/2 poles to a white gum, thence N10.30E 24 poles 15 links to a corner stake between this land and John Wilson's line by marked trees to a stake on the east side of the main road S58E 11 poles S30.30E 13 3/4 poles to a corner willow oak between this land and the lands of George Hope, thence along Hope's line southeasterly 25 1/4 poles to a corner red oak; between this land and said Hope and William Armistead, thence along Armistead's line by marked trees to a corner red oak between said Armistead and James Davis thence along Davis's line S30W 10 poles to a white gum thence N84W 22 poles to a hickory on the line of Mrs. Dewberry thence along her line to the beginning. Wit: James Davis, Thomas C. Amory, James Berry. October 22, 1795 - recorded:Merritt Moore.

207-208 - **Michael King and Ann his wife / John Bains** - October 22, 1795 - Indenture for __ acres: beginning at a corner stob between the land of Michael King and John Wilson running along Wilson's line by marked trees to a corner stump, thence S85W 77 poles to a corner stob between this land and said King's, thence along King's line S11W 7 poles to a corner stob

Elizabeth City County, Virginia 1787-1800

thence S85 1/2E 16 1/2 poles to a corner stob, thence due South 21 poles to a corner stob and from thence to the beginning. Wit: William A.T.Parsons, William Moore, James Saunders. Verification of Ann King's intent to sell. Wit: William Moore, William A.T. Parsons.
October 22, 1795 - recorded:Merritt Moore.

209-210 - **Henriette I.E. Corbier and Miles King / John Sheppard** - October 19, 1795 - Indenture for Peach Tree Fields: beginning at a new made corner pine adjoining Naylor's line and running along the said line to the main road a SE course to Harris's Creek, thence up the said road to a marked gun then along the said road SW to the intersection road from Green Lands, thence up the said road SW to the middle of a brook, thence leaving the road up the swamp as it meanders NE thence NW to three little switch gums a new made corner between Henriette Corbier and the said John Sheppard, thence to the beginning. Wit: Joseph Cooper, John Cooper, James N. Cooper, P.F.A.Sinoire. October 22, 1795 - recorded:Merritt Moore.

211 - **John Seymour / Worlick Westwood, Thomas Wooten, William Dunn** - March 27, 179_ - Indenture of land, slaves and goods as obligation to carry out duties as deputy sheriff to George Booker, Sheriff. Slaves: Judith and children Charolotte and Argile. Wit: Thomas Hatten, John Banks, Hinde Russel, William Badget, Thomas Allen, William Sandy, Blovet Pasteur, Penuel Crook, Edward Rudd, James Gile, John Skinner, Gerrard Seymour. January 22, 1795 - recorded:Merritt Moore.

211-212 - **John Banks and Mary his wife / John Poole** - January 17, 1795 - Indenture for lot of land in Town of Hampton: bound on the east by Queen Street, on the south by Robert Brough, on the north by Rachel Jones. Wit: John Rogers, Henry Jenkins, Edward Face. January 22, 1795 -

Elizabeth City County, Virginia 1787-1800

recorded:Merritt Moore.

213-214 - **Elizabeth Pasteur / Benjamin Pollard of Norfolk** - June 18, 1795 - Indenture for 15 acres: bound beginning on Mill Creek and running N42W 248 poles (line between Cunningham and Mrs. Pasteur) thence N30 44 poles (line between Mrs. Pasteur and William Parish, formerly Rowlands) thence down the Mill Creek to the beginning. (Land used as bond). Wit: William Watkins, Robert Watkins, Blovet Pasteur. July 23, 1795 - recorded:John Moore, D. Clerk.

214-215 - **Barbara Jones** - Will - Susanna Hunter, Mary Herbert, daughters (possibly stepdaughters); Amelia Jones, Anne Jones, Elizabeth Jones, daughters; Thomas Jones,son: Slaves: Moll and James; Pascow Herbert, son-in-law mentioned. Estate called Pembrooke mentioned. Wit: John Applewhaite, George Hope, John Banks verify handwriting. January 22, 1795 - recorded:Merritt Moore.

216 - **Archelaus Yancey / Arthur Henderson** November 14, 1794 - Sale of livestock and furniture as a bond of debt. Wit: William Jennings, William Brough, Robert Sandefer, Robert Elliott, Miles King. January 22, 1795 - recorded:Merritt Moore.

216-217 - **William Smith / John Hoomes of Caroline County** - August 1, 1795 - Indenture for slaves: Harry, Jamy, Lewis, Suckey. Wit: Thomas William Lawson, John Perry. February 26, 1795 - recorded:Merritt Moore.

217-218 - **Mary Courtney Bowrey / Robert Brough of Norfolk** - December 29, 1794 - Sale of slave named Matt was part of William Fraser's estate Wit: William Brough, William Pierce, John Lane, William Jennings. February 26, 1795 - recorded: Merritt Moore.

Elizabeth City County, Virginia 1787-1800

218-219 - **Mary Courtney Bowrey / Robert Brough of Norfolk** - January 1, 1795 - Indenture for lot in Town of Hampton to repay debt: bound on the east by North Street, on the west by lands of the estate of Cornelius Thomas and James Manson, deceased, on the north by lot of estate of John Banks, deceased and on the south by the land belonging to John Roberts, John Jennings Blovet Pasteur and the estate of Robert Buxton, deceased. Wit: William Pierce, John Lane, William Jennings, Job Colton. February 26, 1795 - recorded:Merritt Moore.

220 - **Mary Randle** - Will - October 22, 1794 - John Randle, brother; Elizabeth Randle, niece; Ann Randle, niece mentioned. Wit: Henry Tabb. February 26, 1795 - recorded:Merritt Moore.

220-221 - **Robert Smelt** - Will - May 3, 1795 - Mary Tompkins, daughter; other children not named. Executors: William Ap.Thomas, George Booker. Wit: William Ap. Thomas, James Saunders, Robert Marrow. June 26, 1795 - recorded:Merritt Moore.

221-222 - **Thomas Humphlet** - Will - February 13, 1794 - Elizabeth Humphlet, wife mentioned. Wit: Francis Moss, John Minson, William Burgess. February 26, 1795 - recorded:Merritt Moore.

222 - **Johnson Ross** - Will - October 22, 1795 - Dyannah Ross, sister; Chealy Ross, brother; Ufan Ross, Elizabeth Ross, sisters; Thomas Ross, Frank Ross, Mallory Ross, brothers mentioned. Wit: Richard Smithe, Samuel Rowland, William Rowland. February 26, 1795 - recorded: Merritt Moore.

223 - **Rebecca Dewbre(Dewbrey)** - Will - October 23, 1792 - John Dewbrey, son; Elizabeth Davis, daughter; Thomas N. Dewbre, James H. Dewbre, sons mentioned. Mill and tract of land in Warwick County called Stevens. Wit:

Elizabeth City County, Virginia 1787-1800

John Baines, Mary Wilson, Matthew Baines. February 26, 1795 - recorded:Merritt Moore.

224 - Mary Yancey, widow of Archilaus Yancey / Thomas Wash of Louisa County
February 24, 1796 - Indenture for 500 acres lying in the State of Kentucky. Her husband purchased land from John Duke of Louisa County. No witnesses listed. February 24, 1796 - recorded:M. Moore.

224-225 - Archilaus Yancey - Power of attorney to John Duke, Sr. of Louisa County -
November 3, 1794 - For sale of land in Kentucky upon the Elkhorn creek. Wit: Henry Jenkins, John Jenkins, Rosea Jenkins. February 24, 1796 - recorded:M. Moore.

225 - Archelaus Yancey - Will - February 2, 1795 - Mary Yancey, wife mentioned. Executors: Thomas Fenn, William Pierce. Wit: William Pierce, John Mehollon, John B. Saubot. July 23, 1795 - recorded:Merritt Moore.

226 - Arthur Henderson - Will - 1794 - Ann Boutwell, step-daughter; Ann Henderson, wife; Elizabeth Davis mentioned. Executor Miles King. Land in Fox Hill mentioned. Wit: Samuel Selden, Thomas Latimer, Mary Black. February 26, 1795 - recorded:Merritt Moore.

227-230 - John Reade, deceased - Account of his Estate - Hankins Reade, Executor. Mr. Waller, Edward Moss, William Russell, Joseph Needham, Richard Brown, Lawrence Smith, J. W. Bayley, J. Wood, Henry King, Augustine Moore, Thomas Nelson, William Wise, William Wager, John Skinner, Henry Howard, Thomas Pesceed, Bedford Irvin, William Stevenson, Mr. Everarde, William Reade, General Nelson, Thomas Chisman, Samuel Sandefer, John Dunn, Sandefer Russell, Banister Minson, Thomas Mallicode, George Purdie, Curtis Patrick, Westwood Armistead, John Burnham, John Tazwell,

Elizabeth City County, Virginia 1787-1800

Richard Cary, Benjamin Waller, William Sandefer, John Brodie, William Davenport, John Gunther, William Bailey, Ann Russell, Charles Hansford, Matthew Langston, Wilson Langley orphan of William Allen, Sr., Edward Parish, Mrs. Moss, Mrs. Moore, James Dixon, William Hewitt, Howard Eastin, John H. Norton, Samuel W. Creshy, Callohile Minnis, John Tabb, Nathaniel Burwell, John Kirby, William Marrow, Thomas Lilley, Lockey Collier, William Parriott, Dr. Griffin, Josiah Massenburg, John Hayes, Jaqualin Ambler, Abraham Archer, William Mitchell, William Henderson, James Crandol, Behathland Ridley, E. Dunn, Richard Mackintosh, James Goodwin, John Stevens, William Gooch, Penuel Russell, John Seymour, Cole Diggs, Dr. Powell, William Rogers, Peter Pierce, George Booker, Thomas Webster, Thomas Garrott, Jno. Toomer, Richard Clausell, Gerrard Ridley, Charles Hopson, Servant Jones, Thomas Roberts, Robert Lucas, Sarah Hurst, Thomas Haynes, Col. Dudley Diggs, George Jervis, Moss Armistead, James B. Armistead, Worlick Westwood, Charles Minnis, W. Clurg, Thomas Everard, Merritt Moore mentioned. Subscribers: George Wray, Robert Armistead, Charles Jennings, James Russell, Thomas Archer, James Crandol, John Armistead, James May, Starkey Robinson, John Lowry, Matthew Wells, William Witts. June 26, 1795 - recorded:Merritt Moore.

231-233 - **Lucas Powell and his wife Elizabeth of Amherst County / Abraham Cowper**
August 18, 1794 - Indenture for 50 acres: Lying on Mill Creek, bound on the east by Mill Creek, southwardly by the lands of James Latimer, westwardly by the Glebe Land, northwardly by the land of Joseph Selden. Wit: Will. Cabell, Jr., Wm. Warwick. Affidavit of Elizabeth Powell intent to sell witnessed by Samuel Meredith, William Warwick, and Will. Cabell. February 26, 1795 - recorded:Merritt Moore.

233-234 - **Robert Reade and his wife Elizabeth**

Elizabeth City County, Virginia 1787-1800

of Halifax County / George Purdie, Jr. of York County - January 12, 1795 - Indenture for 41 acres: bound on the north by the main road leading to Warwick , on the east by the lands of Robert L. Russell, on the south by the land of William Garrow, on the west by the land of Thomas Robinson. This is land given to Robert Reade by will by his father. Wit: Cole Robinson, H. Reade, John Kirby, Samuel Cook. June 26, 1795 - recorded:Merritt Moore.

234-235 - **Michael King and Ann his wife / Worlick Westwood** - January 22, 1795 - Indenture for 1/4 of lot and tenament in Town of Hampton: lying on the east side of the main street leading to the wharf and bounded northerly by the lots of Joseph Needham and southwardly by the lot of John Hunter which said tenement and lot of land Henry King, deceased formerly lived on and by his last will devised it equally divided between his surviving children. Wit: John Bright, Charles Jones, Thomas Lowry, Joseph Cooper, Jr., John Shepherd, Samuel Bland. June 26, 1795 - recorded:Merritt Moore.

235-237 - **William Westwood / John Stith Westwood** - January 2, 1795 - Indenture for 205 acres: beginning at a corner gum in the Free School swamp, thence N5W 75 poles to a willow tree in the said swamp on the York road N50E 34, W57E 28, N79E 43 3/4 to a gum tree on the Main road N56,E160 to a locust tree on Mrs. Jones ditch S85 E 46, S74E 32, S79 to the cross roads W96 to a bridge on the said road thence up the swamp as it meanders to an oak tree in the said swamp thence S2W 6 to a marked pine tree between the lands of said Worlick Westwood and the lands of Miles King S66 1/4 to a gum tree on James Swamp thence up the said swamp as it meanders to a corner chestnut tree, thence N36, W60 to a corner little gum tree in the Free School swamp thence down the said swamp to the beginning. Wit: John Wray, John Banks, John

Elizabeth City County, Virginia 1787-1800

Harper, Edward Face, James Banks, John Banks, Jr., Charles Jennings, John Bright, Miles King. Burying ground excepted. June 26, 1795 - recorded:Merritt Moore.

237-238 - **Augustine Moore** - Will - November 9, 1793 - Anne Moore, wife; William Moore, Augustine Moore the younger, Merritt Moore, John Moore, Ann King, Jane Sweney, children; George Booker, son-in-law mentioned. Wit: Roscow Parsons, Jenny Parsons, Mary Parsons. June 26, 1795 - recorded:Merritt Moore.

238-239 - **John Hunter** - Will - December 26, 1794 - Susannah Hunter, wife; Mary Ann Barbary, John Hunter, William Jones Hunter, Thomas Hunter, children. Slaves: Kate, Betty, Minerva, Dann mentioned. Wit: Miles Cary, Thomas Jones, William Davenport. Codicile - Barbara Jones, mother mentioned. June 26, 1795 - recorded: Merritt Moore.

240-241 - **Rebecca Dewbre** - Appraisement of estate - November 29, 1794 - Household goods, tools, furniture. Slaves: Fanny, Judith. Appraisers: William Allen, John Allen, John Baines. June 26, 1795 - recorded:Merritt Moore.

241 - **Gerrard Seymour** - Appraisement of estate - July 24, 1794 - Livestock, furniture. Appraisers: James Smith, William Guy, William Smith. July 23, 1795 - recorded:Merritt Moore.

242-243 - **Roe Cowper and Jane his wife / Thomas Payne** - September 29, 1794 - Indenture for 2 acres: Commonly known as Ferry Point, opposite Hampton called Irvins Point: the south corner beginning at the water side and running N80E 7 feet south of William Green house to a marked sycamore tree from thence about a north course along high water mark to the main creek, thence as the river runs to the beginning place. Wit: James Cowper, John Cowper, Sarah Cowper. July 23, 1795 - recorded:Merritt Moore.

Elizabeth City County, Virginia 1787-1800

243-244 - **Worlick Westwood and Hannah his wife / George Bates** - July 23, 1795 - Indenture for lot and tenement in Town of Hampton: bound on the south by land of David Brodie, west and north Worlick Westwood, east by Kings Street then running westwardly from the north corner of the said house ___ feet or as far as the lot formerly extended. Wit: Richard H. Hurst, James Banks, Jr., John Banks, Jr. July 23, 1795 - recorded:Merritt Moore.

245-246 - **Henry Jenkins / Samuel Burkette** November 23, 1794 - Articles of Agreement: for rent of old field for 21 years. Wit: James Burke, Penuel Sands, James Cunningham. July 23, 1795 - recorded:Merritt Moore.

246 - **Judy Saunders** - Will - July 2, 1794 - Robert Saunders, Mary Saunders, Ann Saunders, Elizabeth Saunders, James Saunders,children; Mary Saunders, James Saunders Wilson, Ann Wilson, grandchildren, George Booker; slaves: Will, Nanny mentioned. Wit: William Davis, Ann Booker. July 23, 1795 - recorded:Merritt Moore.

247-248 - **John Cary** - Will - October 28, 1794 Susannah Cary, wife; Miles Cary, Hannah Armistead, Betsy Allen, Gile Armistead, John Cary, Judith Robinson, Susannah Nathanial, Robert Cary, children; Robert Cary, brother; Richard Cary and Miles Cary of Warwick County. Capt. John Parsons, mentioned. Slaves: George, Joe, Judy, Jack, Lydia mentioned. Land in Charles Parish, Lower York County mentioned. Wit: J. M. Galt, John Kerby, William Brown. July 23, 1795 - recorded:Merritt Moore.

248-249 - **Worlick Westwood / Miles King** September 22, 1795 - Indenture for 27 acres of Little England. Lately property of Capel and Osgood Hanbury, British subjects, sold by Moss Armistead escheator by virtue of two acts of Assembly. September 24, 1795 - recorded:Merritt Moore.

Elizabeth City County, Virginia 1787-1800

249-250 - **Robert Armistead, son of William / William Allen** - Sale of slaves of Edward Armistead, deceased. Martha Armistead mentioned. Wit: Blovet Pasteur, Miles King, John Bright. September 24, 1795 - recorded: Merritt Moore.

250 - **Johnson Tabb** - Will - January 6, 1795 Henry Tabb, brother; Mary Harwood Tabb and unnamed infant, children mentioned. Wit: William Smith, Mary Tabb. September 24, 1795 - recorded:Merritt Moore.

251 - **Nathaniel Whitaker (formerly from Canan, Massachusetts) physician** - Will - January 20, 1795 - Sarah Whitaker, wife; Jonathan Whitaker, Williame Smith Whitaker, children mentioned. Wit: Benjamin Bryan, George Hope, Minson T. Proby, John Jennings. Memorandum: Mrs. Sarah Trowbridge mentioned. September 24, 1795 - recorded:Merritt Moore.

252 - **John Page / Miles King** - April 15, 1795 Indenture of land and slaves in trust for Elizabeth King Mallory, spinster daughter of Col. Francis Mallory, deceased. Tract at Buckroe mentioned. Slaves: Lewis, Cuff, and Joe. Wit: John Bright, Martha King, John A. Wray, William Allen. September 24, 1795 - recorded:Merritt Moore.

253 - **George Booker, Sheriff / William Brough** September 26, 1794 - Receipt for slaves and livestock taken from William Mannis to satisfy debt to Robert Brough. Slaves: Caleb, Sylvia Wit: James N. Cowper, John Latimer, Joshua King, Richard Rowland, John Rogers. October 22, 1795 - recorded:Merritt Moore.

253-254 - **Robert Armistead** - Appraisement of estate - February 19, 1793 and April 28, 1794 after death of Mrs. Armistead. Slaves: Fanny, Rachel, Sally, Peter Mossom, Bess and 3 children, Pat and child, Peter, Sam, Ned, Bob,

Elizabeth City County, Virginia 1787-1800

Sue and 3 children, Wiley, Sarah and child, Hannah and 3 children, Jeofry, Jack, Lockey, Sylvia, Old Peter, Milly, Phillis, Little Fanny, Beck and child, Betty. Appraisers: William Armistead, Jr., Thomas Allen, Thomas B. Armistead.

255-257 - **Robert Armistead** - Sale of estate - January 2, 1795 - Mrs. Armistead, Shelden Moss, William Kerby, John Skinner, Augustine Moore, William Seymour, Doctor Applewhaite, Starkey Robinson, John Sandrum, John Wilson, B. Smithe, John Cary, Thomas B. Armistead, Thomas Willings, Robert Armistead, John Applewhaite, George Booker, W. Westwood, Capt. William Armistead, Willis Wilson, Thomas Hatton, Richard Smithe, Thomas Minson, Charles Jones, Penuel Sands, Miles King, David Smelt, Thomas Kerby, John Willings, William King, Jr., Samuel Burkett, Thomas Allen, Jno. Willings, William Moore, John Sclater, James Cook. July 23, 1795 - recorded:Merritt Moore.

258-259 - **Barbara Jones** - Inventory of estate - December 29, 1794 - Household goods, livestock. Slaves: Sam, Lucy, Mill, Sally and children, Fanny, Fener, Gift, Andeen, Ned, Little George, Old George, Old Dick, Little Dick, Daniel, James. Boat: <u>Charles</u>; Boat: <u>Jude</u>. Appraisers: Charles Jennings, William Kerby, William Brough. July 23, 1795 - recorded:Merritt Moore.

260 - **Archelus Yancey** - Appraisement of estate - Household goods, tools, livestock. Appraisers: William Latimer, William Latimer, Jr., John Shepherd. September 24, 1795 - recorded:Merritt Moore.

261-262 - **William Moore and Mary his wife / Augustine Moore** - September 21, 1795 - Indenture for 50 acres: bound on the northwest by William Hylton, on the southeast by Augustine Moore, deceased. Wit: John Moore, Michael King, Willaim Ap. T. Parsons.

Elizabeth City County, Virginia 1787-1800

Acknowledgement of Mary Moore.
September 24, 1795 - recorded:Merritt Moore.

263-265 - **Thomas Blane of London / Charles Young (of London but sailing to Virginia)** - March 19, 1793 - Power of Attorney. Verified by letters from James Sanderson, Lord Mayor of London and Robert Holmes. February 24, 1795 - recorded:Merritt Moore.

266-267 - **Sarah Jennings of Norfolk County; Mary Jennings, her daughter; Charles Jennings, her son / George Hope** - July 21, 1795 - Indenture for lot in Town of Hampton where the late William Jennings lived: bound east and south by the lands of George Hope, west by North Street, north by the lines of the land of Captain Joseph Meredith. Wit: William Guy, Joseph Meredith, James Smith, William Green. Also signed by Polly Ellmore Jennings.
October 22, 1795 - recorded:Merritt Moore.

267-268 - **Wilson C. Wallace and Catharine his wife / John Parish, pilot** - February 24, 1796 - Indenture for lot and house in Town of Hampton Wit: Bartlett Field, W. Moore, Miles Cary, William Armistead. February 24, 1796 - recorded:Merritt Moore.

269 - **Thomas Jigetts, bricklayer / James Burk** - July 27, 1795 - Indenture for 65 acres: adjoining the land said Burk and bound on Saltfords Creek. Wit: John Bright, Miles King, John Stith Westwood. October 22, 1795 - recorded:Merritt Moore.

270-272 - **William Rowland and Mary his wife / William and Mark Parish** - October 1, 1795 - Indenture for 10 acres of land on Mill Creek: beginning at a large stone on Mill Creek and running N42W 244 poles as per marked trees to the intersection of an old line on the orginial tract running N30E, down the said N30E five poles thence leaving the said line and running

Elizabeth City County, Virginia 1787-1800

S43E 242 poles to Mill Creek shore thence along the said shore as it meanders to the beginning. A general access road must be left on the shore. Part of will of Margaret Mossom. Surveyed by John A. Wray. Wit: Richard H. Hurst, James Banks, Samuel Selden, Edward Face. Acknowledgement of Mary Rowland. January 28, 1796 - recorded:Merritt Moore.

272-273 - **Jacob Wray / George Wray** - October 28, 1795 - Indenture for 310 acres called Ashton Mannor and all that goes with it including the following slaves: Ned, Ben, Winney, Rachel, Charlotte, Plymouth. Wit: George Booker, Miles King, W. Moore, Thomas Kerby, Samuel Watts. January 28, 1796 - recorded:Merritt Moore.

273-274 - **Jacob Wray / John Ashton Wray** - October 28, 1795 - Indenture for 50 acres on Saltfords Creek Road adjoining the lands of Mallory Ross and all that goes with it including the following slaves: James, Tom, Nan, Matilda, Frances, Poplar, Nanny, Jane. Wit: Miles King, George Booker, W. Moore, Samuel Watts, William Thomas Kerby. January 28, 1796 - recorded:Merritt Moore.

275-276 - **Edward Face / Richard Hawkins Hurst** - October 5, 1794 - Indenture for lot in Town of Hampton: bound by lands of John Hicks, Casar Tarrent, Edward Face and the Hampton River. Frances Face mentioned. Wit: William _____, John Laine, John Beane. Worlick Westwood and George Wray witness the acknowledgement of Frances Face to sale. January 22, 1795 - recorded:Merritt Moore.

276-277 - **John Parish, pilot / Wilson Wallace and Catharine his wife** - February 24, 1796 Indenture for 75 acres: That parcel of land whereon the Mill Ordinary formerly called stands: beginning at a pine stump at the Creek running southerly to the head of the lands

Elizabeth City County, Virginia 1787-1800

adjoining Eatons Free School, thence westwardly to the Lands of John Fields still bounded by the said Free School Land thence northerly along the said John Fields land to the Creek or marsh and from thence to the beginning. Wit: W. Moore, John Moore. February 24, 1796 - recorded:Merritt Moore.

277-278 - **Thomas Parsons of Williamsburg / Robert Greenhow of Williamsburg** - June 20, 1795 Indenture for 249 1/2 acres in Elizabeth City County bound by the lands of Johnson Tabb, deceased; Jacob Wray, John Parson, deceased. This land was purchased by Sarah Parsons of Samuel Roberts and willed to Thomas Parsons. Wit: George Greenhow, James Davenport, William Hunter. January 28, 1796 - recorded:Merritt Moore.

279 - **William Westwood and John Stith Westwood / Miles King** - July 28, 1795 - Indenture for 96 acres: Land willed to the Westwoods by Merritt Westwood: beginning at the crossroads running west 96 poles to the bridge in the road thence from the bridge up the middle of the swamp with its meanderings to a corner oak in the middle of the swamp thence south 71 poles to the intersection of a swamp thence down the said swamp as it meanders thence N3E 96 poles to an intersection line thence S87E 108 poles to a pine on Celey's road thence down the road to the beginning. Wit: John Bright, William Kerby, Joseph Bushell, Minson Proby, John Page. February 24, 1796 - recorded:Merritt Moore.

280 - **William Brough / Robert Brough of Norfolk** September 28, 1795 - Sale of livestock and slaves: Caleb and Sylvia, once owned by William Manice and his wife Grace Elizabeth Manice. Wit: George Bates, John Page, Minson Proby, John Bright. January 28, 1796 - recorded: Merritt Moore.

280-281 - **William Manice and his wife Grace**

Elizabeth City County, Virginia 1787-1800

Elizabeth and the Commonwealth of Virginia / Robert Brough of Norfolk - September 26, 1795 - Sale of slave: Jesse, who was part of estate of William Fraser and willed to Grace Elizabeth Manice. Wit: John Needham, Thomas Kerby, William Jennings, John Latimer. January 28, 1796 - recorded:Merritt Moore.

281-282 - **William Manice and Grace Elizabeth his wife / William Brough** - September 26, 1795 - Sale of slaves: Caleb and Sylvia. Wit: John Rogers, James N. Cooper, John Latimer, Joshua King. January 28, 1796 - recorded: Merritt Moore.

282-283 - **John Stores / Charles Stores** - December 26, 1795 - Indenture for 17 acres: joining Joseph Bushell and Benjamin Stores, running a straight course to a pine a corner tree near the road from thence along the road between William Armistead down to a pine tree to a corner between William Stores from thence a straight course between Charles Stores to a mark gum from thence a straight course to the beginning place. Wit: Joseph Cooper, James N. Cooper, Thomas Minson. January 28, 1796 - recorded:Merritt Moore.

283-284 - **Sarah Burt, widow of Richard Burt / Elizabeth Humphlet and Rebecca Minson** - Sale of slaves: Joan, Jupiter, Kate. Wit: John Skinner, William Gooch. February 24, 1796 - recorded: Merritt Moore.

284-285 - **Elizabeth Humphlet / John Minson** September 2, 1795 - Articles of agreement on possession of slaves of Minson's wife. Elizabeth Burt, Rebecca Burt, Sarah Burt and slaves: Rachell, Peg, Tom, Delphia, Joan, Milly, Kate, Jupiter mentioned. Wit: Samuel Skinner, William Gooch. February 24, 1796 - recorded:Merritt Moore.

285 - **James Bayley** - February 8, 1796 -

Elizabeth City County, Virginia 1787-1800

Agreement on settlement of part of his father's estate. John Bayley, George Booker, Joseph Needham, Miles King, William King, William Redwood, John Stith Westwood, Walter Bayley, William Armistead Bayley mentioned. Wit: Miles King, John Bright, John Minson. February 24, 1796 - recorded:Merritt Moore.

286 - **John Bayley** - appraisal and division of slaves of his estate - February 3, 1796 - William King, John Stith Westwood, William Redwood, James Bayley, Walter Bayley and slaves: George, Andrew, Rubin, Jupiter, Charles, Mun, Bob, James, Beck and child mentioned. Appraisers: Miles King, Joseph Needham, George Booker. February 24, 1796 - recorded:Merritt Moore.

287 - **John Stith Westwood / William Redwood** - February 3, 1796 - Receipt of payment for slaves from estate of John Bayley. Wit: Miles King, George Booker, Thomas B. Armistead. February 24, 1796 - recorded:Merritt Moore.

287 - **John Stores** - Will - December 26, 1795 - Charles Stores, brother mentioned. Wit: Joseph Cooper, James N. Cooper, Thomas Minson. February 24, 1796 - recorded:Merritt Moore.

288 - **Job Colten** - Will - August 28, 1787 - Ann Colten, wife; Samuel Colten, son; Robert Brough and his sister, Amelia Brough mentioned. Wit: Miles King, Charles Jennings, W. Kerby, John Ashton Wray. February 24, 1796 - recorded: Merritt Moore.

289 - **Chevers Elliott** - Appraisement of estate June 25, 1795 - Household goods and livestock. Appraisers: John Cooper, Thomas Latimer, James N. Cooper. February 24, 1796 - recorded: Merritt Moore.

289 - **Elizabeth Russell** - account of sale of

Elizabeth City County, Virginia 1787-1800

estate - March 9, 1792 - James Tompkins, David Spruce, Lazarus Wood, Mrs. Weymouth, James Davis, William Allen, John Robinson. February 24, 1792 - recorded:Merritt Moore.

290 - **James Williams** - Appraisement of estate _____, 1790 - Slaves: Jefry, Pegg, Judy, Mingo, Jack, Nanny, Rachell, Tiller, Liza, Hanner. Also livestock and household goods. Appraisers: Thomas Fenn, John Sheppard, William Pierce. February 24, 1796 - recorded:Merritt Moore.

291 - **James Stores** - Accounting of Estate - George Booker, Miles King, Worlick Westwood mentioned. February 24, 1796 - recorded:Merritt Moore.

291 - **John Wilson, Jr.** - Appraisement of Estate Tools, household goods, livestock. Appraisers: John Banes, John Wilson, John Allen. February 24, 1796 - recorded:Merritt Moore.

292-293 - **John Wilson** - Sales of Estate - James Davis, Mary Wilson, Benjamin Buck, Charles Jones, Thomas Allen, Lazarus Wood, William Allen, Sr., Robert Marrow, John Banes, John Dewbry, John Garrow, William Mallory, Miles King, John Williams, Robert Armistead. February 24, 1796 - recorded:Merritt Moore.

293-294 - **Jacob Wray / George Wray, his son** - October 29, 1796 - Indenture for lot in Town of Hampton: bounded by the lots of Joseph Needham and George Wray. Wit: Thomas Kerby, James Banks, Jno. Banks, Pascow Herbert. April 28, 1796 - recorded:Merritt Moore.

294-295 - **Samuel Selden and Susanna his wife / Joseph Meredith** - April 28, 1796 - Indenture for lot in Town of Hampton: bounded northwardly by the land of Wilson Curle, deceased, eastwardly by Hampton Creek, southward by the land of Joseph Meredith and westwardly by Wine

Elizabeth City County, Virginia 1787-1800

Street. Land was willed by Joseph Selden. April 28, 1796 recorded:Merritt Moore.

296 - **Ann Jones** - Will - February 6, 1796 - Thomas Jones, brother; Miles Cary; Amelia Jones, sister mentioned. Plantation called Low Fields. Wit: Miles King, John Applewhaite. April 28, 1796 - recorded:Merritt Moore.

297-298 - **Mary Tarrant** - Will - _____ 1790 - Frances Bayley, sister; William Bayley, Charles Bayley, Thomas Bayley, Servant Ballard, John Ballard, nephews; Rebecca Baker, niece; George Wray, John Ashton Wray, James Latimore, Miles King mentioned. Wit: Pascow Herbert, William King, Samuel Healy. April 28, 1796 - recorded:Merritt Moore.

298 - **Hannah King** - Will - March 22, 1796 - Judith Curle King, daughter; Elizabeth Owings, granddaughter; Joshua C. King, Henry Jenkins King, John C. King, William King, sons. Slaves: Nancy, Jack and Violet. Wit: Henry Jenkins, Pascow Herbert. April 28, 1796 - recorded: Merritt Moore.

299-300 - **Roe Cowper / William Green** - June 23, 1796 - Indenture for 1/2 acre land: beginning at a stake on Hampton River and running S87E east 24 poles, intersecting a direct line drawn from the corner of William Green's house at the distance of 7 feet therefrom to a ditch and road near the sycamores thence S1W 10 feet thence south 82 degrees west 29 poles between the said William Green and William Brown running into the Hampton River, thence up the said river as it meanders to the beginning. Wit: John A. Wray, Richard H. Hurst, William Lowry. June 23, 1796 - recorded:Merritt Moore.

300-301 - **Thomas Paine and Dorothy his wife / William Green** - June 23, 1796 - Indenture for 158 square poles of land: beginning at a stake in the Hampton River the dividing line between

Elizabeth City County, Virginia 1787-1800

John Been and the said William Green and running S88E 18 poles 18 links thence S1W 7 poles 16 links on back line next the road, thence N87W 24 poles adjoining the said William Green's 1/2 acre, thence up the river as it meanders. Wit: John A. Wray, Richard H. Hurst, William Lowry. June 23, 1796 - recorded:Merritt Moore.

302 - **Thomas Jones / Anne Rosetta Borrowdale** April 1, 1796 - Receipt for payment from James Borrowdale's estate. Wit: James Smith, William Bayley. June 23, 1796 - recorded:Merritt Moore.

302-303 - **William Harper of Portsmouth / John Harper, Jr.** - March 9, 1796 - Indenture for lot in Town of Hampton: bound on the north by Robert Dobson, on the south by George Hope, on the east by Hampton Creek on the west by the Main Street. (the land where Mrs. Purkinton now lives). Wit: John Britain, John Banks, Miles King, Richard H. Hurst. June 23, 1796 - recorded:Merritt Moore.

304 - **John Robinson** - Appraisement of estate - October 2, 1794 - Household items. Slaves: Sam, Ned, Moll, Jenny, Fanny, Grace, Old Jack, Billy, Jupiter, Joe. Appraisers: Samuel Selden, Richard Williams, Arthur Henderson. June 23, 1796 - recorded:Merritt Moore

305-306 - **Robert Dobson and Mary his wife, formerly Mary Minson / Miles King** - December 6, 1795 - Indenture for 57 acres: beginning at a stake on the north side of Mill Creek and running thence by a line of marked trees northwest until it intersects the northwest line of the whole tract, thence with that line to the corner thence by a line of ancient marked trees to the creek, thence with the creek to the beginning. Wit: John Harper, Robert Brown, John Bright, William Kerby, George Hope, Warren Hopkins, Worlick Westwood. June 23, 1796 - recorded:Merritt Moore.

Elizabeth City County, Virginia 1787-1800

307 - **James Ottley / his children** - March 22, 1796 - Gift of possessions to Ann Ottley, Coverton Ottley, Sammuel Ottley, James Ottley, John Ottley, Thomas Ottley. Slave: Sally. Wit: William Seymour, Charles Jones, Thomas Robinson, William Allen. Signed by James Ottley and Elizabeth Ottley. June 23, 1796 - recorded: Merritt Moore.

308 - **William Manice / Eleanor Bowry** - December 12, 1795 - Sale of slaves to satisfy bond and debt that William Manice has with William Joseph Dufour. Slaves: Jenny, Jesse, Caleb, Sylvia. Wit: Benjamin Bryan, William Joseph Dufour, John Russell, William Latimer. July 28, 1796 - recorded:Merritt Moore.

309 - **Edward Delaney** - Will - April 21, 1796 - Elizabeth Delaney, wife; Edward Delaney the younger, Pamelia Delaney, John Delaney, children mentioned. Wit: John Perry, John Parish, Richard Gilliam. July 28, 1796 - recorded:Merritt Moore.

309-310 - **Robert Elliott** - Will - December 5, 1793 - Martha Elliott, Ann Buxton, sisters; William Elliott, Harry Elliott, Thomas Elliott, brothers; George Booker. Slave: Charles and George mentioned. Wit: Joseph Cooper, Thomas Latimer, John Latimer. July 28, 1796 - recorded:Merritt Moore.

311-312 - **Francis Riddlehurst** - Will - May 7, 1796 - Francis Riddlehurst Bright, John Bright sons of Robert Bright and Mary Bright; Ann Toomer, daughter of Thomas Butte and Ann Butte, Susanna Selden, wife of Samuel Selden; Hannah Drew, widow of William Drew, Priscilla Johnson, Mary Carleton, George Hope, Sr., Pascow Herbert. Slaves: Billy, Hannah, Hampton mentioned. Wit: Wilson Wallace, J. Hardiman, James Cunningham. July 28, 1796 - recorded: Merritt Moore.

Elizabeth City County, Virginia 1787-1800

313-314 - **David Brodie / Benjamin Street** - November 20, 1796 - Indenture for lot in Town of Hampton: bounded westwardly and northwardly by the lots of Worlick Westwood, southwestwardly by a vacant piece of land and eastwardly by the Main street leading to the wharf. Land where Dr. John Brodie, deceased, lived. Wit: Joseph Meredith, George Wray, John A. Wray, William Banks. July 28, 1796 - recorded:Merritt Moore.

314 - **Miles King / Edward Face** - September 21, 1796 - Indenture for 3 1/2 acres: part of a tract purchased by William Wager and beginning at the road on Edward Face's line and running northwardly by along the said road to a marked tree thence westwardly to the line of the said Edward Face, thence southerly down a little branch to the beginning place. September 22, 1796 - recorded:M. Moore.

315-316 - **Worlick Westwood / Edward Face** - August 18, 1796 - Indenture for lot in Town of Hampton: bounded from the corner of Kings Street as far on main street leading to the wharf to the line of George Bates then westwardly along the said Bates line leading from the north end of his house to the west corner of the said Bates line thence turning down the said Bates line nearly south to Brody's line then westerly to a corner stone, then leading northwardly to Queen's Street thence eastwardly to the beginning. Wit: Michael King. Acknowledgement of Hannah Westwood. October 27, 1796 - recorded:M. Moore.

317 - **Catherine Wallace, wife of Wilson C. Wallace** - April 9, 1796 - Acknowledgement of sale of land to John Parish. Wit: Worlick Westwood, Robert Armistead. September 22, 1796 - recorded:M. Moore.

318 - **William Hicks and Frankey his wife / John Rogers** - January 29, 1793 - Indenture for lot

Elizabeth City County, Virginia 1787-1800

in Town of Hampton: bounded southerly by Queen Street, northerly by Robert Brough's lot, westerly by John Rogers lot and easterly by Robert Buxton's lot. Wit: William Ap. Thos. Parsons, William Moore, Minson T. Proby. September 22, 1796 - recorded:M. Moore.

318 - **William Brough, Robert Armistead, Robert Armistead, Jr.** - Ordered by court to make an audit of the records. Report given September 22, 1796:M. Moore.

319-320 - **John Hutchings / Miles King and George Booker, Trustees** - January 23, 1796 - Indenture for brick house and lot in Town of Hampton: adjoining the lot of Francis Riddlehurst. Wit: Miles Cary, John Bright, William Pierce, Thos. B. Armistead, Robert Armistead, William Brough. September 22, 1796 - recorded:Merritt Moore.

320-321 - **William King / John Curle King** - August 22, 1796 - Indenture for 50 acres of land formerly in the possession of his late father where the new house stands. Bound by the land of Mr. Edward Cowper, the land of John Curle King, and the main road dividing the said land and John Curle Kings from Capt. Pascow Herbert. Wit: Sheldon Moss, Charles Jennings, William Jennings. Acknowledgement of Elizabeth King. Wit: William Moore, Michael King. September 22, 1796 - recorded:M. Moore.

322-323 - **Robert Armistead, William Armistead, Miles King / Robert Brooke, Governor of the Commonwealth of Virginia** - September 22, 1796 - Bonds for office of sheriff for Robert Armistead.

323 - **Robert Sandefer, Elizabeth Sandefer / Worlick Westwood, Sheriff** - August 6, 1796 - Receipt for payment from estate of father. Molly Sandefer mentioned. Wit: John Bright, Miles King. September 22, 1796 - recorded:M.

Elizabeth City County, Virginia 1787-1800

Moore.

324 - **William Badgitt** - Accounts of estate with Thomas West and Josiah Massenburg - Roby Coke, Robert Brough, Miles King, Dr. Valentine Hamm, William Sandy, John Skinner, Samuel Thomas, Matthew Langston, Rosea Fields, Thomas Patrick, Samuel Dewbry, Johnson Tabb, Augustine Moore, Mr. Burnham, Thomas Dewbry, William Diggs, Bartlett Fields, Ellison Skinner. Examiners: Miles King, Thomas Jones, John Perry. October 27, 1796 - recorded:Merritt Moore.

325 - **Mary Tabbs** - Will - December 17, 1795 - Priscilla Tabb, Mary Tabb, daughters; John Tabb, deceased husband; Johnson Tabb, Henry Tabb, sons of John Tabb; Thomas Tabb, son of Mary Tabb. Slaves: Jacob, Patty, Peter, Daniel, Hannah, George, Grace, Frank, Sarah mentioned. Wit: Miles King, Jenny Parsons. October 27, 1796 recorded:M. Moore.

326 - **Thomas Jones and Pascow Herbert / Commonwealth of Virginia** - Bond office of coroner for Thomas Jones. October 27, 1796 - recorded.

326-327 - **William Latimer, Sr. / Thomas Latimer, son of William Latimer, Jr., deceased** - July 25, 1796 - Indenture for 50 acres called Boutwell. William Latimer, Easter Whiten Latimer, Sarah Latimer and slave, James mentioned. Wit: William Brough, Samuel Selden, Samuel Watts, Jr., Thomas Jones. October 27, 1797 [sic] - recorded:M.Moore.

327-328 - **James Baker and Rebecca his wife / Miles King** - September 24, 1796 - Indenture for 92 acres: adjoining lands of Samuel Selden, William Armistead, and John Sheppard. Wit: W. Seymour, Richard Cary, W. Lane, William Hunt, Robert Armistead, William Seymour, Jr., Thomas Fenn. January 26, 1797 - recorded:M. Moore.

Elizabeth City County, Virginia 1787-1800

329 - **Richard Williams and James Waller Williams / Richard Routen** - January 26, 1797 - Indenture for 25 acres: bound by lands of William Latimer, William Lewis and Harris Creek. No witnesses. January 26, 1797 - recorded:M. Moore.

330-331 - **Edward Allen and Elizabeth his wife / Miles King** - September 3, 1796 - Indenture for 2 tracts of land: (1) 182 1/2 acres: bound on the river and running westerly along the line of the lands purchased by Miles King of Nelson Miles Cary and Elizabeth Allen and running up to the land of Robert Armistead's orphan commonly called Black Ground, thence northerly along the said Armistead line to Robert Armistead son of Westwood line, then along the said line easterly to William Armistead son of Mosely line thence along the said line to Robert Armistead's orphan line thence along the said line easterly to a cove that leads into Back River and thence along the river southerly to the beginning place. (2) 50 acres being what Henry Allen purchased of John Bayley and bound by land of Robert Armistead's orphan, Worlick Westwood and the lands Miles King purchased of Wilson Miles Cary. Wit: John Bright, Thomas Jones, William Armistead. January 26, 1797 - recorded:M. Moore.

331-333 - **Rachel McClurg, James Smith and Rachell his wife, Jane King of Prince William County / Worlick Westwood** - November 17, 1797 - Indenture for lot and tenament in Town of Hampton: bound by the lot of Joseph Needham northerly, westwardy by King's Street, southwardly by Oswald's lot and eastwardly by Hampton River. Wit: John Bright, William Watkins, John S. Westwood, R. Armistead, Henry Tabb. January 26, 1797 - recorded:M. Moore.

333-334 - **Robert Brough / Ann Colton** - August 30, 1796 - Receipt for sale of slaves: Davy, Sam, Andrew sons of Sue, and old Judy.

Elizabeth City County, Virginia 1787-1800

Doctor Job Colton mentioned. Wit: William Brough, George Booker. January 26, 1797 - recorded:M. Moore.

334 - **Ann Colton / Robert Brough** - October 30, 1796 - Sale of slaves: Davy, Sam, Andrew, Old Judy. Wit: George Massenburg, Jerome Dubond, William Brough. January 26, 1797 - recorded:M. Moore.

335 - **Thomas Whitby Dewbre / James Davis** - January 17, 1797 - Indenture for 100 acres: willed by John Dewbre to Thomas. Wit: Miles King, William Skinner, John Bright. January 26, 1797 - recorded:M. Moore.

336 - **William Latimer / Miles King** - January 17, 1797 - Indenture for 200 acres: called Fox Hill Ridge (deducting the 50 acres sold to Thomas W. Dewbre adjoining the lands of Thomas Bayley's estate, Lewis's land and Andrew Bulley and Arthur Henderson. George Latimer, Thomas Latimer mentioned. Wit: James Davis, Thomas W. Dewbre, John Bright. January 26, 1797 - recorded:M. Moore.

337 - **William Latimer / Thomas W. Dewbre** - January 16, 1797 - Indenture for 50 acres: [Fox Hill] beginning on a creek and running a southwardly course on Bayley's line as far as will make the 50 acres so as to take in the channel of two coves to make the 50 acres as compact as can be. Wit: Miles King, James Davis, John Bright. January 26, 1797 - recorded:M. Moore.

338 - **James Tompkins** - Appraisement of estate October 27, 1796 - Livestock, tools, gun. Appraisers: Augustine Moore, William Armistead, Augustine Moore, Jr. January 26, 1797 - recorded:M. Moore.

338 - **John Daws** - Will - January 3, 1797 - Gilbert Daws, Ezekial Daws, John Daws,

Elizabeth City County, Virginia 1787-1800

Bartholomew Daws, William Daws, sons; Rachell Daws, Sarah Daws, daughters mentioned. Wit: John Skinner, Thomas Webster Bullock. January 26, 1797 - recorded:M. Moore.

339 - **Charles Jennings guardian of John and Henry Robinson / George Minson** - November 21, 1796 - Lease of plantation for four years. Wit: Robert Dobson, Elizabeth C. Wallace. January 26, 1797 - recorded:M. Moore.

339-340 - **Capt. John Hunter** - Appraisement of estate - July 8, 1795 - Household itmes. Slaves: Violet, Betty, Sally and child, Cate, Dan, Minerva. Appraisers: William Brough, William Kerby, William Smith. February 23, 1797 - recorded:M. Moore.

341 - **John Reade and Robert Read of the county of Halifax / George Purdie, Jr. of the county of York** - January 12, 1795 - Indenture for 131 acres: bounded on the north by Wises mill pond on the east by the lands of Robert Armistead, on the south by the land of Joseph Nichols, on the west by the land of Martha Armistead. Some of the land was willed to the Reade's by their father John Reade. Wit: Cole Robinson, John Kerby, John Sclater, John Russell. June 25, 1795 - recorded:M. Moore.

341-343 - **Rebecca Dewbry** - Account of sale of estate - December 1794 - James Davis, David Saunders, John Dewbry, John Bains, William Seymour, John Allen, John Wilson, Thomas Dewbre, Robert Maney, Capt. Miles King, John Williams. June 26, 1795 - recorded:M. Moore.

343 - **John Walker** - December 16, 1795 - Gives power of attorney to George Wray. Wit: John Rogers, Thomas Kerby, William Kerby. April 27, 1797 - recorded:M. Moore.

344-345 - **George Wray for John Walker / John Jennings** - March 11, 1797 - Indenture for 131

Elizabeth City County, Virginia 1787-1800

acres: On Mill Creek beginning at the head of a branch between John Page and land of John Walker running as by marked trees N42W 160 poles to a corner Walker and Mead's blazed trees thence S32W 112 poles as by marked trees between Mead and Walker to an intersection on Rudd's line corner between Mead and Walker thence S45E 240 poles between Rudd and Walker as by marked trees into Mill Creek River thence up the said creek as it meanders to a cove on said Mill Creek between the said Walker and Page thence up the said cove as it meanders to the head of the branch to the beginning. Wit: John A. Wray, John Page, Charles Jennings, Saml. Watts, Jr. witnesses. April 27, 1797 - recorded:M. Moore.

345-346 - **Rebecca Dewbry** - Settlement of estate Edward Face, John Wilson, George Booker, Merritt Moore, James Davis, David Brodie, Robert Brough, John Dewbry, Mary Mallory. Wit: George Wray, John Bright, William Kerby. February 23, 1797 - recorded:M. Moore.

347-348 - **John Jennings / George Wray** - March 11, 1797 - Indenture for 131 acres: See previous entry for details. Wit: John A. Wray, John Page, Charles Jennings, Samuel Watts, Jr. April 27, 1797 - recorded:M. Moore.

348 - **John Banks, Sr. / John Banks, Jr.** - April 27, 1797 - Deed of gift: Blacksmith shop and quarter of lot where on it stands. Wit: Thomas Jones, John Harper, Michael King. April 27, 1797 recorded:M. Moore.

349 - **Thomas Kerby** - Will - October 28, 1796 - William Kerby, brother mentioned. Wit: Miles King, Charles Jennings. April 27, 1797 - recorded:M. Moore.

349 - **William Goddin** - Will - December 26, 1795 Thomas Watts mentioned. Wit: B. Sheppard Morris, Ann Morris, Samuel Watts. April 27,

Elizabeth City County, Virginia 1787-1800

1797 - recorded:M. Moore.

350-351 - **Henry Jenkins / David Smelt** - Indenture for lease of small house and old field: bound beginning at Cary's ditch thence easterly to a pine tree, thence easterly to a ravan thence easterly to a pine at the swamp side thence along the swamp to a sassafras thence to a pine tree thence to a chesnut tree thence to another pine tree thence to a ravan thence to a pine large tree corner thence to a little dogwood bush on the side of Cary's ditch thence on the line along Cary's ditch to the beginning. Restrictions on types of wood to be cut and seed to be sown. Wit: Penuel Sands, William Cunningham, James Cunningham. April 27, 1797 - recorded:M. Moore.

351 - **James Naylor Cooper / Jack** - March 23, 1797 - Emancipation of Jack. Wit: Thomas Jones, John Jennings. June 22, 1797 - recorded:M. Moore.

352 - **John Pauls / Robert Pauls** - April 8, 1797 Indenture for lot in Town of Hampton: bound northwardly by land of Richard Barron, deceased, westwardly by King Street, southwardly by Queen Street opposite John Banks and eastwardly by the lot formerly sold by John Pauls to Basill Smith. Wit: John Banks, Edward Face, James Ballard, Richard H. Hurst. June 22, 1797 - recorded:M. Moore.

353 - **Benjamin Bryan** - Will - May 28, 1797 - William Bryan, son; Sarah Marchant, Mary Bryan, Patsy Bryan, daughters; Thomas Jones mentioned. Wit: Jno. Applewhaite, Minson T. Proby, Thomas Jones. June 22, 1797 - recorded:M. Moore.

353-354 - **Ann Moore, widow of Augustine Moore / William Moore her son** - December 23, 1796 - Indenture for plantation left to her by her husband's will. Wit: Augustine Moore, Jr., Ann Moore, Mary Moore, John Moore, Augustine Moore.

Elizabeth City County, Virginia 1787-1800

July 27, 1797 - recorded:M. Moore.

355 - **Thomas Paine and Dorothy his wife / John Been** - July 27, 1797 - Indenture for lot of land on east side of Hampton River beginning at a stake or stone on Hampton River the corner, and running S69E 16 poles thence S1W 2 poles 21 links thence N88W west 18 poles 18 links into Hampton River between John Been and William Green thence up Hampton River to the beginning containing 98 3/4 square poles cut from the land of Thomas Paine. Witnesses not listed. July 27, 1797 - recorded:M. Moore.

356-358 - **Joseph Meredith and his wife Elizabeth / Robert Armistead -** April 24, 1797 - Indenture for lot in Town of Hampton: bound southward on Queen Street, westward by the lot of David Davis, northward by the lot of William and Mary Colledge, eastward by Kings Street. Worlick Westwood, Robert Armistead mentioned. Wit: George Hope, Jno. Banks, George Hope, Jr. July 27, 1797 - recorded:M. Moore.

358 - **William Armistead and Elizabeth his wife and Frances Armistead / Worlick Westwood -** March 18, 1797 - Indenture for 12 acres: that lies on the north side of the main road leading to Sawyers Swamp beginning at a gum tree corner of the said Westwood land and running thence a straight line to a pine tree standing on the road side thence with the road until it intersects the said Westwood line thence with this line to the beginning. Wit: Blovet Pastuer, Richard B. Servant, George Hope, Jr., John Harper. July 27, 1797 - recorded:M. Moore.

359-360 - **Richard Dixon** - Account of sale of estate - Elizabeth Dixon, Mary Dixon, Richard Hurst, Miles King, John Banks, John Lane, John Been, Worlick Westwood, John Williams, George Booker, Arthur Henderson, James Smith, John Pauls, William Kerby, William Brough, George Latimer, John A. Wray, Henry Durant, Thomas

Elizabeth City County, Virginia 1787-1800

Paine, Charles Conniers, Henry Jenkins. September 28, 1797 - recorded:M. Moore.

360-361 - **Francis Pool** - Account of sale of estate - January 6, 1795 - John Been, William Brough, Fanny Bains, Thomas Paine, James Cunningham, William Stores, Eppa Dunoway, Richard Hurst, Christiana Williams, Fanny Pool, Edward Rudd, George Booker, Thomas Bulley, William Bushell, Thomas Lewis, Samuel Selden, William Guy, Richard Williams, Willis Wilson, John Skinner, James Latimer, Charles Been, William Dobbins, Charles Jones, Joseph Bushell, Benjamin Stores, William Latimer, Jr., William Manice, William Bayley, Thomas Wellings, Doctor Whitaker, Peter Black, John Pool, Richard Barnaba, William Brown, Charles Stores, Edward Bulley, William Armistead, Johnson Mallory, Samuel Burket, William Pearce. September 28, 1797 - recorded:M. Moore.

362 - **James and Judy Sanders** - Account of sale of estate - December 4, 1794 - John Sanders, Willis Wilson, John Dewbre, John Moore, John Wilson, George Booker, James Sanders, William Allen, James Davis, John Presson, Mary Sanders, Robert Sandefer, Robert Maney, Eppa Dunoway, William Brown, John Randell, Mr. Stevenson, Mrs. Bell, Mr. Skinner, David Spruce, Doctor Applewaite, Mr. Nettles, Robert Armistead, Alex. Maney, Charles Jones, Robert Smelt. September 28, 1797 - recorded:M. Moore.

363-364 - **John James Ward / Robert Brough / William Brough** - March 14, 1797 - Indenture for lot in Town of Hampton: bound on the east by North Street, on the west by lots belonging to heirs of Cornelius Thomas and James Manson, on the north by a lot lately belonging to John Banks and on the south by lands belonging to John Rogers, Blovet Pasture and John Jennings. Also two slaves: Ben and Phoebe and other goods. Deed of Trust - Indenture used as security for debt. Wit: John Harper, Robert

Elizabeth City County, Virginia 1787-1800

Dobson, Blovet Pasture, Charles Pasture. September 28, 1797 - recorded:M. Moore.

364-365 - **James Latimer / John Davis** - June 28, 1797 - Indenture for 15 acres: beginning at a marked gum for a corner tree of the whole land and running thence by a line of marked trees S41E 172 poles to the creek, thence up the creek 14 poles to a stump and stake thence N41W till it intersects the back line being the line of a tract of land formerly belonging to William Brough thence with this line to the beginning. Wit: John Cooper, John Bright, Miles Cary. September 28, 1797 - recorded:M. Moore.

365 - **John Bright** - Noncupative will - Samuel Bright, brother; Francis Bright mentioned. September 28, 1797 - recorded:M. Moore.

366 - **John Moore / William Moore / Mary Shield Hollier Moore** - March 3, 1797 - Indenture for slaves: Tim, Peter, Florah, Pender, Judy, Esther, Phobe, Dinah as well as land and other goods to be held in trust. Wit: Michael King, William Landrum, Augustine Moore, Jr. September 28, 1797 - recorded:M. Moore.

366-368 - **Wilson Curle Wallace and Catherine his wife / William Allen** - March 8, 1797 - Indenture for 75 acres: that tract of land whereon the Mile Ordinary formerly as called stands beginning at a pine stump at the Creek running thence southerly to the head of the lands adjoining Eaton's free school thence westward to the lands of John Fields still bound by the said school land, thence northerly along the said John Fields land to the creek or marsh and from thence to the beginning. Wit: James Smith, James Burk, R. Armistead, Miles King, William Kerby, George Wray. October 1797 - recorded:Merritt Moore.

368-369 - **Ann Rosetta Wray / Jacob Wray, heir at law to John Ashton Wray** - September 29, 1797

Elizabeth City County, Virginia 1787-1800

-Indenture for 616 acres in Dinwiddie County, 50 acres in Elizabeth City County, one house in Hampton. Wit: Worlick Westwood, Charles Jennings, Jno. S. Westwood, Robert Armistead, Richard H. Hurst. October 1797 - recorded: Merritt Moore.

369-371 - **Wilson Davis and Mary his wife of Isle of Wight County / Thomas Lowry** - July 19, 1797 - Indenture for 45 acres on the south side of Harris Creek beginning at the bank of the ditch nearly opposite James Naylor running a direct south course by a heap of stones and so on by an old ditch to an elm thus to a sapling pine thence to another sapling pine thence to a large gum on the road leading to Fox Hill from thence running south twelve degrees west to a _____ adjoining the lands of William Armistead from thence N12W along the said Armistead line to a small gum on the road aforesaid from thence along the said road on the said Armistead line to a corner pine at the school house where it joins the other lands of the said Robert Wallace from thence running along the road leading to Greenland to an oak thence to a white oak thence to Naylors bridge from thence running N45E to the corner of the ditch ajoining the lands of the said Robert Wallace whereon William Jones formerly lived from thence this said ditch ending at the place begun. Bannister Minson, Philip Cowper mentioned. Wit: Miles King, George Booker, William Armistead, William Lowry, Robert Lowry. February 1798 - recorded:Merritt Moore.

371-372 - **John Cooper, executor of Jane Naylor Watts / James Naylor Cooper** - February 21, 1798 Indenture for 137 acres on Harris Creek. Wit: Johnson Mallory, Thomas Lowry, Thomas Latimer. February 1798 - recorded:Merritt Moore.

372-373 - **John Applewhaite / Miles King** - January 31, 1797 - Mortgage of livestock, household goods and slave Esther. Wit: Charles

Elizabeth City County, Virginia 1787-1800

Jennings, James Latimer, Joseph Selden. September 1797 - recorded:Merritt Moore.

373-374 - **James Bayley** - Appraisement of estate Household goods and livestock. Appraisers: Thomas B. Armistead, Shelden Moss, John Skinner. October 1797 - recorded:Merritt Moore.

374 - **John Bayley** - Appraisement of estate - Household goods and livestock. Appraisers: Thomas B. Armistead, Bartlet Field, Sheldon Moss. October 1797 - recorded:Merritt Moore.

375 - **Charles L. Boush and Prudence his wife of the borough of Norfolk / John Rogers** - October 1, 1797 - Indenture for lot in Town of Hampton: bound on the east by a piece of land lately purchased by John Rogers from William Hicks, on the West by Wine Street, on the north by a lot belonging to the heirs of Cornelius Thomas and on the south by Queen Street. Wit: Joe Boyce, Thomas Newton, Jr., Robert Boush. October 1797 - recorded:Merritt Moore.

376 - **Jean Watts** - Will - April 27, 1797 - Samuel Watts, son; Euphan Russell, granddaughter; Sarah Lunsford, daughter; Elizabeth Buxton, Sarah N. Buxton, granddaughters; John Cooper, grandson. Slaves Judith and Rachel. Wit: Samuel Watts, Jr., Ann Sheppard. January 1798 - recorded:Merritt Moore.

376-377 - **Ann R. Wray / John Page** - September 28, 1797 - Indenture for lot in Town of Hampton: bound on the north by Mrs. ___'s lot, on the east by Hampton River, on the south by the lot of Thomas Jones, Jr., on the west by King's Street. Wit: Johnson Mallory, M. E. Chisman, William Armistead, George Wray. October 1797 - recorded:Merritt Moore.

377-379 - **Robert Armistead Petition of writ ad Quod Damnum** - September 30, 1796 - Petition to

Elizabeth City County, Virginia 1787-1800

create a new water grist mill and dam lying on the head of Back River in the counties of Elizabeth City and York and commonly called Wises Water Grist Mill. He wishes to abutt his dam against the lands of Charles Collier. Land is described as being on one side of the North Branch of Back River. John Robinson, George Purdie, Jr., Penuel Russell, Elizabeth Armistead, Charles Miles Collier, Lockey Collier. Jurors: Shelden Moss, James Davis, John Cooper, Thomas B. Armistead, Henry Tabb, William Allen, John Skinner, Davis Saunders, Robert Sandefer, John Allen, William Allen, Jr., John Bains. October 26, 1796 - recorded: Merritt Moore.

380-382 - **Moss Armistead** - Account of estate by William Armistead - Elizabeth Pasture, George Booker, Dr. James McClurg, Captain Herbert Davis, Richard Cary, Miles Cary, Blovet Pasture, Robert Brough, Rachael Jones, Wilson Curle, Mary Curle, Thaddious Freshwater, Polly Jennis, Matthew Wright, Nancy Armistead, Polly Armistead, Johnson Tabb, Samuel Selden, Miles King, Ralph Littlepage, Ann Armistead, Starkey Robinson, John Seymour, Pricilla Armistead, David Spruce, Mary Woods, John Moss, John Rogers, John Cary, William Armistead, Slaves: Hannah, Pegg, Milly Joe, Charles, Davy, Esther, Nanny George, Moll, Sue and two children, Lewis. October 1797 - recorded:Merritt Moore.

383 - **Joseph Meredith** - Will - March 12, 1797 - Elizabeth Margaret Meredith, wife; Joseph Meredith the younger, Elizabeth Margret Meredith the younger, son and daughter. Wit: John Spooner, Minson Proby, Ann Toomer, Mary Proby, Elizabeth Bean. January 1798 - recorded: Merritt Moore.

383-384 - **Fanny Smith** - Will - March 19, 1797 - Mary Smith, sister. Slave, Nancy. Wit: Samuel Rowland, John Douglass, John Simpson. January 1798 - recorded:Merritt Moore.

Elizabeth City County, Virginia 1787-1800

384- **Jacob Wray, father of John Aston Wray and Ann Rosetta Wray / Robert Brough** - October 2, 1797 - Sale of slaves: Nan, Matilda, Old Nanny, Jenny. Wit: Thomas Jones, George Latimer. January 1798 - recorded:Merritt Moore.

385-386 - **John Page and Elizabeth his wife / Thomas Jones** - January 8, 1798 - Indenture for lot in Town of Hampton: bound on the north by Mrs. McCan, south by Thomas Jones, west by King Street, east by the Hampton River. Wit: Merritt Moore, Henry Gerace Letuz, M. K. Letuz, James Cooper, William Smith, James Burke. January 1798 - recorded:Merritt Moore.

386-387 - **Thomas Allen / Edward Face** - December 27, 1797 - Receipt of horses to cover debt. Wit: Robert Armistead, James Davis. February 1798 - recorded:Merritt Moore.

387-388 - **Casar Tarrant** - Will - February 19, 1797 - Desires that after his wife's death that his property be sold in order to purchase the freedom of his daughter Liddy. Nancy Tarrant, Sampson Tarrant, children - mentioned. Wit: John Hicks, David Hicks, Thomas Chisman, John Russell. September 1797 - recorded:Merritt Moore.

388-389 - **Worlick Westwood and Hannah his wife / George Bates** - July 24, 1795 - Acknowledgement of Hannah Westwood to sale of property. February 1798 - recorded:Merritt Moore.

389-390 - **Abraham Cowper / Miles King** - August 15, 1797 - Indenture for 50 acres of land on Mill Creek and adjoining the lands of James Latimer and Joseph Selden as security for debt. Wit: Charles Mallory, John Brittain, James Cunningham, R. Armistead. February 1798 - recorded:Merritt Moore.

390 - **Samuel Bland** - Appraisement of estate -

Elizabeth City County, Virginia 1787-1800

January 26, 1798 - Household goods. Appraisers: John Cooper, Thomas Fenn, Thomas Latimer. February 1798 - recorded:Merritt Moore.

391 - **James Tompkins** - Accounting of estate by Michael King - January 26, 1797 - Robert Armistead, Miles King, Rachael King, James Smelt, Major Parsons, George Booker, John Skinner, Robert Marrow, William Landrum. February 1798 - recorded:Merritt Moore.

391 - **William Godwin [Goddin]** - Sale of estate - Small amount of household goods. February 1798 - recorded:Merritt Moore.

392 - **Frazer Stores** - Account of sale of estate by Robert Armistead - July 4, 1797 - Robert Armistead, Miles King, William Pierce, Thomas Dewbry. February 1798 - recorded:Merritt Moore.

392-393 - **William Watkins** - Account of sale of estate by Robert Armistead - February 5, 1798 - John Rogers, Robert Watkins, William Hodge, Polly Watkins, Jno. Been, Abraham Cowper, Richard Rowland, W. Bedingfield, John Been, Charles Jennings, George Hope, Miles King, John Skinner, Capt. Herbert. William Watkins' widow purchased his pilot boat. February 1798 - recorded:Merritt Moore.

393-394 - **William Bayley / Thomas Jones, Jr.** - July 1, 1797 - Indenture for land and slaves. Wit: Miles King, James Smith, John Bright, Richard H. Hurst. January 25, 1798 - recorded: Merritt Moore.

395-399 - Pages are blank.

400-401 - **Samuel Barron and his wife Elizabeth / Nathaniel Bedenfield** - February 28, 1798 - Indenture for a lot in the Town of Hampton: beginning at the corner of Back Street running along the said street to Hunt's lot thence down the said Hunts to the creek thence up the creek

Elizabeth City County, Virginia 1787-1800

to Curle's line thence along Curles line to the beginning. Wit: John Applewhait, Thomas Minson, Worlick Westwood, Jr., Richard H. Hurst. Acknowlegement of Elizabeth Barron. June 28, 1798 - recorded:Miles King.

401-402 - **Charles Yancey of Louisa County / David Yancey** - April 12, 1798 - Charles granting power of attorney to David. Wit: R__ C. Crawford, Polly Yancey. June 28, 1798 - recorded:Worlick Westwood, Jr.

402 - **George Wray, Attny for John Walker of Kentucky / John Jennings** - Release of debt. June 28, 1798 - recorded:Worlick Westwood, Jr.

403 - **Miles King, executor for Arther Henderson / David Muray** - November 6, 1797 - Indenture for 75 acres adjoining the lands of Andrew Bully and Miles King. Had been purchased of Ben Wooten. Wit: Ed. Ballard, John Russell, William Kerby. June 28, 1798 - recorded:Worlick Westwood, Jr.

404 - **Worlick Westwood and Hannah his wife / Thomas Watts** - November 30, 1797 - Indenture for lot in Town of Hampton: William Graves on the west, James Cunningham and Edward Delaney on the south, Edward Face on the east and Queen Street on the north. Wit: Worlick Westwood, Jr., Jno. L. Westwood, Richard Hurst. June 28, 1798 - recorded:Worlick Westwood, Jr.

405-406 - **Elizabeth Pasteur / William Ham (Hame, Hamm)** - April 23, 1798 - Indenture for 15 acres: on Mill Creek: bound on Mill Creek running N42W 248 poles (line between Cunningham and Mrs. Pasteur) thence N30E 17 poles thence S42E 244 poles (line between Mrs. Pasteur and William Parish formerly Roeland) thence down the Mill Creek to the beginning. Wit: Blovet Pasteur, Worlick Westwood, George Hope. June 28, 1798 - recorded:Worlick Westwood, Jr.

Elizabeth City County, Virginia 1787-1800

406-407 - **Nathaniel Bedingfield** - Will March 19, 1798 - Mary Bedingfield, wife; William Bennett (of Surry), John Hardyman, Captain Samuel Ellis. Slaves: Tiller, Dianna, James. Wit: John Britain, J. Banks, Timothy Baker. June 28, 1798 - recorded:Worlick Westwood, Jr.

407-408 - **J. Thomas Silverthorn** - Will March 16, 1798 - Sabastin Silverthorn, son; Elijah Jervis, possible son-in-law or grandson; John Silverthorn, George Silverthorn, sons; Susannah Jervis, daughter; John Nickolson mentioned. Wit: Jno. Nicholson, Thos. Nicholson, Jas. Halaway. June 28, 1798 - recorded:Worlick Westwood, Jr.

409-410 - **Samuel Watts** - Will - December 26, 1797 - Thomas Watts, son; Daniel Routten, mentioned; Samuel Watts the younger, son; George Walker, William Williams, mentioned; Thomas Watts, son; Mary Bright, Susanah Haynes, Ann Jennings, Sarah Williams, Elizabeth King, daughters; Charles Jennings - mentioned Slaves: John, Jacob, Pegg, Agnes, Dinah, Peter, John Matthew, Sue, Ned, James, Fillis, Nan, Sam Wit: James N. Cooper, Thomas Latimer, Thomas Lowry, John Been. July 28, 1798 - recorded: Worlick Westwood, Jr.

410-411 - **John Banes (Baines)** - Will - February 15, 1798 - Matthew Baines, John Banes the younger, William Banes, Henry Banes, Richard Banes. Wit: James Davis, John Allen, Fanny Baines. July 27, 1798 - recorded.

411-412 - **James Bayley - Court decree for division of slaves from estate** - Mary King, William A. Bayley, John S. Westwood. Slaves: Old Jenny, Beck and child Sally. Subscribers: Charles Jennings, Edward Face, Jno. Banks. July 27, 1798 - recorded:Worlick Westwood, Jr.

412-413 - **Thomas Minson of Harris Creek / Miles**

Elizabeth City County, Virginia 1787-1800

King - November 28, 1798 - Indenture for debt. Includes house, slaves, furniture. Wit: Charles King, John Harper, Richard H. Hurst, William Armistead, James Cunningham, Worlick Westwood, Jr. July 27, 1798 - recorded:Worlick Westwood, Jr.

414-415 - **John Davis / Miles King** - November 29, 1798 - Indenture for debt. Includes 15 acres bounded on the lands of the late Samuel Servant and the land of Bennett's orphans and on Mill Creek and headed on the land of James Lattimer. Wit: John Bright, Richard H. Hurst, Miles Cary, Thomas Jones, James Cunningham, Abraham Cowper. July 27, 1798 - recorded:Worlick Westwood, Jr.

415-416 - **Miles and Martha King / William Armistead, Sr.** - June 22, 1798 - Indenture for 65 acres: bounded on the north by the land of Miles King, on the south by the River or Creek, on the east by the lands of William Armistead, on the west by the land of Samuel Selden. July 27, 1798 - recorded:Worlick Westwood, Jr.

416-417 - **Joseph Meredith** - Appraisement of estate - July 3, 1798 - Household goods. Slaves: Frank, George, Rose, Toney, Sale, Joe, Dick, Miles, Tom, Jim, Silvey, Rodey. Appraisers: Charles Jennings, George Hope, Minson T. Proby. July 27, 1798 - recorded.

417-418 - **William M. Holland** - Account of estate Miles King - James Davis, Doctor Applewhaite, Robert Armistead, John Allen, William Mallory, John Wilson, Johnson Tabb, John Robinson, Mr. Fields, Colonel Langhorne, Michael King, John Drewery. Wit: Charles Jennings, Joseph Needham, John Perry. Mary M. Holland - signature. July 27, 1798 - recorded: Worlick Westwood, Jr.

419 - **Peter Manson / Robert Brough of Norfolk** - September 27, 1798 - Bill of sale for slave:

Elizabeth City County, Virginia 1787-1800

Nancy. Wit: Samuel Watts, John Randle. September 27, 1798 - recorded:Worlick Westwood, Jr.

420 - **William Armistead, Jr.** / **John Allen** - July 26, 1798 - Indenture for 50 acres: lying on the east side of Sawyer Swamp Road and adjoining the land of Miles King and George Wray on the north and on the east by William Armistead, Sr., and on the south by George Hope and the main road. Wit: R. Armistead, Aug. Moore, George Booker. September 27, 1798 - recorded:Worlick Westwood, Jr.

421-422 - **Samuel Thomas and his wife Sarah** / **William Williams of Warwick County** - July 14, 1798 - Indenture for 50 acres: known as Luke Ridge bound as follow: heading the lands of Robert Sandefur on the northwest, running from thence a south course on the lands of Mrs. Yeargin from thence running the said course to the lands belonging to Mr. Curle and from thence a strait course to the beginning place. Wit: Michael King, William Allen, William Landrum. July 14, 1798 - recorded:Worlick Westwood, Jr.

423-424 - **David Pierce of Norfolk** / **Warren Hopkins** - January 2, 1792 - Indenture for lot in Town of Hampton: on North Street extending from a lot of Hezekiah Warde being the south boundary unto the lot of Joseph Selden being the north boundary, the street being the east boundary and the lot of Joseph Selden being the west property. Wit: George Hope, J. Smith, Servant Ballard, Robert Brough, William J. Hunger, John Rogers. January 23, 1793 - recorded:Worlick Westwood, Jr.

424-425 - **Charity Harper** - Acknowledgement of sale of land to Cesar Tarrant - September 18, 1798. Wit: James Brough, Charles Jennings. September 27, 1798 - recorded:Worlick Westwood, Jr.

Elizabeth City County, Virginia 1787-1800

426-427 - **William Lattimer / James Howell** - January 9, 1798 - Indenture for 25 acres known as Averas: lying on the north side of Harris Creek. Beginning at a branch that makes out of Harris Creek a southwest course to a white gum and from thence to another white gum, and from thence a straight course to a cedar post and from thence a southeast course to a corner pine which parts the line between Mr. Curles and from thence down the side line an east course to Harris Creek again which line joins the said William Lattimers land that he purchased of Charles White. Wit: Samuel Selden, William King, George Latimer. September 27, 1798 - recorded:Worlick Westwood, Jr.

427-428 - **Rebecca Whittaker / Worlick Westwood** - May 28, 1798 - Indenture for 2 lots in Town of Hampton: bound on the west by King Street, the North by W. Westwood, the east by Wine Street, the south by Richard Barron, deceased. Wit: Henry Elliott, Robert Armistead, Worlick Westwood, Jr. September 27, 1798 - recorded:Worlick Westwood, Jr.

428 - **Richard Backhouse** - Receipt for his payment - April 1798 - To Servant and A. T. Dixon for payment on plantation called Saltfords Creek containing 235 acres. Wit: Samuel Cunningham. September 27, 1798 - recorded:Worlick Westwood, Jr.

429-430 - **Ann Dixon** - Acknowledgement of sale to Richard Backhouse - July 17, 1795 - Sale of Saltford Creek plantation: bound in the south and southwest by the lands of Wilson Miles Cary, in the west by William Digges, in the north west by William Gooch, in the north by lands formerly owned by Anthony Hawkins and the mill marsh, on the east by Saltfords Creek. Wit: Samual Vaughan, Samuel Donovill. September 27, 1798 - recorded:Worlick Westwood, Jr.

Elizabeth City County, Virginia 1787-1800

430-431 - **Mary Curle** - Appraisement of estate - August 15, 1795 - Slave: Venus. Household goods, livestock. Wit: William Latimer, Jno. Nicholson, William King. September 27, 1798 - recorded:Worlick Westwood, Jr.

431 - **Col. Francis Mallory** - Account of estate - Slaves: Peter, Nelly, Fanny, Dan. Molly Mallory, Mary Mallory mentioned. Wit: Charles Jennings, George Hope, William Brough. October 25, 1798 - recorded:Worlick Westwood, Jr.

432-435 - **Mary Mallory** - Account of estate - Amounts due for sundry items. Various credits. Balance due to Miles King. Wit: Charles Jennings, George Hope, William Brough. October 25, 1798 - recorded:Worlick Westwood, Jr.

436-437 - **Col. Francis Mallory and Mary Mallory** -Sale of estate - February 1789 - William Smith, Servant Ballard, Jno. Banks, Robert Brough, Wilson Wallace, John Parrish, William Sandy, Robert Armistead, Jno. Perry, William Jennings, Miles King, James Burke, Warren Hopkins, Jno Applewhaite, William Parsons, Thomas Lattimer, Col. Cowper, Augustine Moore, William Pierce, Johnson Tabb, George Sweeney, George Booker, Jno Skinner, William Houghton, Willis Wilson Cleaves, James Bayley, William Allen, Thomas Allen, Robert Halloway, Pascow Herbert, James Dixon, James Davis, James Guy, Bartlett Field, John Nettles, Frances Riddlehurst, Jno Been, Nathan Yancey, Thomas Minson, Thomas Humphlet, George Wray. October 25, 1798 - recorded:Worlick Westwood, Jr.

438 - **Francis and Mary Mallory** - Division of estate - November 23, 1798 - John Page, Elizabeth Page, H. G. Latues, Mary Latues, Charles Mallory. Slaves: Lucey, Peter, Cate, Zilphan, Kate, Mun, Tom, David, Chelcey,

Elizabeth City County, Virginia 1787-1800

Jamees, Ned, John, Moses, Billy, Old Sarah, Rachel, Betty, Luckey, Hariot, Pebby, Hannah, Sue, Judey, Sally, Will, Tom, Old Hanna. Wit: Charles Jennings, George Hope, William Brough. October 25, 1798 - recorded:Worlick Westwood, Jr.

438 - **Worlick Westwood / Worlick Westwood, Jr.** May 21, 1798 - Deed of gift: lot in Town of Hampton: bound north by Worlick Westwood, east by Proby, south by Barron, west by King Street. October 25, 1798 - recorded:Worlick Westwood, Jr.

439-440 - **Francis Tarrant and Elizabeth his wife of Norfolk / Robert Armistead** - April 7, 1798 - Indenture for lot in Town of Hampton: bound west by Wine Street, north by Joseph Meredith, east by John Pool and Rachael Jones and William Armistead, south by Peter Manson. Wit: Samuel Selden, James Wood, George Randolph. October 25, 1798 - recorded:Worlick Westwood, Jr.

440 - **Mary Curle / Miles King** - April 20, 1798 - Sale of slaves: Will, Sam, Hannah, Lettice, Betty and child Maria. Wit: William Allen, John Wood. October 25, 1798 - recorded: Worlick Westwood, Jr.

441 - **John Williams** - Will - August 13, 1797 - Nancy Williams, wife; Mary Williams, daughter; Capt. Edward Ballard. Slave: Sarah. Wit: Richard H. Hurst, John Britain, Sarah Barron. October 25, 1798 - recorded:Worlick Westwood, Jr.

442 - **Jno. Weymouth** - Account of estate by Jas. Burke - Miles King, Johnson Tabb, Col. Westwood, G. Booker, Jno. A. Wray, Jno. Wilson, Wm. Smith. Wit: Charles Jennings, William Smith, Worlick Westwood. Octobter 25, 1798 - recorded:Worlick Westwood, Jr.

Elizabeth City County, Virginia 1787-1800

443 - **Miles King / Wilson Miles Cary** -
April 28, 1798 - Indenture of land and lot.
Wit: Thomas Watts, Abraham Cooper. October 25,
1798 - recorded:Worlick Westwood, Jr.

444 - **Martha King** - Acknowledgement of sale of
lot to John Moore - Wit: Michael King, William
Brough. December 27, 1798 - recorded:Worlick
Westwood, Jr.

445 - **Martha King** - Acknowledgement of sale of
land to James Barrondale - Wit: Michael King,
William Brough. December 27, 1798 - recorded:
Worlick Westwood, Jr.

446-447 - **Miles King and Martha his wife /
Thomas Jones, Jr.** - April 28, 1798 - Indenture
for 300 acres: lying on Sawyer Swamp Road and
adjoining land of John Allen, William Mallory,
Westwood Armistead, and George Wray. Land was
willed to Martha King by her father Thomas
Kerby. Wit: Michael King, William Brough.
Acknowledgement of Martha King of sale.
December 27, 1798 - recorded:Worlick Westwood,
Jr.

448 - **Merit Moore** - Will - April 15, 1798 -
Mary Wise mentioned. William Moore, John
Moore, brothers. Slave Rachel is to be freed.
Wit: Augustine Moore, Jr., Ann Mallory Moore.
December 27, 1798 - recorded:Worlick Westwood,
Jr.

449 - **Margaret Bell** - Appraisement of estate -
Household items, livestock. Appraisers -
Charles Collier, Samuel Thomas, Thomas
Robinson. December 27, 1798 - recorded:Worlick
Westwood, Jr.

449-450 - **Martha Armistead** - Will -
November 15, 1788. Mary Bell, Martha Tompkins
Armistead, granddaughters; William Allen,
Patrick Walker, Francis Mennis Armistead,
Samuel Armistead, grandsons; Miles King

Elizabeth City County, Virginia 1787-1800

mentioned. Wit: M. M. Robinson, Everard Robinson. Codicil dated January 1795. February 28, 1799 - recorded:Worlick Westwood, Jr.

451-452 - **Abraham Tennis and Joshua Tennis of York County / Thomas Baker Armistead** - January 14, 1799 - Indenture for 172 acres: bounded by lands of Miles King easterly and southerly, lands of Thomas Fenn westerly and the water of Back River northerly. Wit: Jno. Nicholson, Aaron Tennis, Thomas Fenn. February 28, 1799 - recorded:Worlick Westwood, Jr.

452-453 - **Miles King and Pascow Herbert as executors of Barbara Jones / John Minson** - July 7, 1798 - Indenture for 40 acres: on the head of Saltfords Creek formerly belonging to John Jones, deceased. Bound southerly by the land of Willis Skinner, deceased, westerly by the land of Anthony Hawkins, deceased, northerly by the land of Wilson Curle, deceased and easterly by the land of Richard Bast, deceased. Wit: Samuel Cunningham, Abraham Cooper, James Baker. February 28, 1799 - recorded:Worlick Westwood, Jr.

453 - **William Lattermore (Latimer) / Larrance Hains, Susana Hains, Patsy Hains, Samuel Hains** January 29, 1799 - Deed of gift: Slaves: Frank, Diner, George, Antony. Wit: Charles Jennings, Richard H. Hurst. February 28, 1799 - recorded: Worlick Westwood, Jr.

454 - **Thomas Baker Armistead and Ann his wife; Mary Seymour of Norfolk; John Shepard / Abraham Tennis and Joshua Tennis of York County** - January 14, 1799 - Indenture for 172 acres: bound by lands of Miles King easterly and southerly, Thomas Fenn westerly, waters of Back River northerly. Wit: Thomas Fenn, Aaron Tennis, Jno. Nicholson. February 28, 1799 - recorded:Worlick Westwood, Jr.

Elizabeth City County, Virginia 1787-1800

455-456 - **Matthew Banes (Bains) and Mary his wife / James Davis** - December 15, 1798 - Indenture for 19 acres inherited from Mary Wood: not identified. Wit: R. Armistead, Ann Sanders, John Sandifer. February 28, 1799 - recorded:Worlick Westwood, Jr.

456-457 - **Samuel Thomas and Sarah his wife / William Allen** - November 19, 1798 - Indenture for 100 acres: bound by William Williams easterly, Thomas B. Armistead and Robert Maney southerly, and by a line of marked tree which divides the premises from the lands of the said Samuel Thomas westerly and northerly including the plantation whereon James Bell now lives. Wit: James Davis, James Bell, John Weymouth. February 28, 1799 - recorded:Worlick Westwood, Jr.

458-459 - **Samuel Shield as administrator for estate of John Kerby, deceased and his heirs: Elizabeth Kerby, William Marrow and his wife Mary; Humphrey Harwood and his wife Martha; William Kerby and his wife Sarah; Elizabeth Kerby, Richard Kerby, Lucy Kerby, John Kerby / William Hylton** - May 3, 1798 - Indenture for 16 acres: bound by lands of William Mallory on the southside of the road leading towards the free school on Back River and on the edge of the lands late the property of George Wythe (the said 16 acres of land having been formerly part of the Wythe's tract and having been exchanged by Margaret Wythe for 16 acres and 2/3 lying upon old Poquoson River which were conveyed by Hannah Francis to the said Margaret Wythe who transfered the within mentioned 16 acres of land to the said Hannah Francis who was the great-grandmother of Mary, the wife of Edward Cuttillo, who conveyed the said 16 acres of land to the said John Kerby, deceased. Wit: John Chisman, William S. Wills, Starkey Robinson. February 28, 1799 - recorded:Worlick Westwood, Jr.

Elizabeth City County, Virginia 1787-1800

460 - **Angelique Henriette Lousteaud Herrone Widon Corbieres and Miles King / Alexander Joseph Alphonse David Beauregard** - October 15, 1798 - Indenture for 250 acres: remainder of plantation Erroll. One hundred acres known as Peach Tree Fields was sold to John Shepard. Wit: John Cooper, Samuel Bright, Thomas Latimer, William Armistead, Thomas Lowry, William Moore, William King. February 28, 1799 - recorded:Worlick Westwood, Jr.

461 - **Augustine Moore / Meritt Moore** - March 2, 1799 - Bill of sale: slaves: Rachell, Ben, Willtshire and household items. Wit: William Moore, Augustine Moore, Jr. April 25, 1799 - recorded:Worlick Westwood, Jr.

462 - **William Elliott / Henry Howard Elliott** - December 4, 1798 - Bill of sale: slave: Sall, and livestock. Wit: Samuel Selden, James Burk, William Cooper. April 25, 1799 - recorded: Worlick Westwood, Jr.

462 - **Miles King / Thomas Minson, Jr.** - April 15, 1799 - Deed of Release: Ann Boutwell mentioned. April 25, 1799 - recorded:Worlick Westwood, Jr.

463 - **James S. Ballard** - Will - January 21, 1788 - Edward Ballard, Francis Ballard, brothers; Sarah Ballard, niece. Wit: John Seymour, William Dunn. April 25, 1799 - recorded:unsigned.

463 - **Jacob Wray / Thomas Dixon** - April 26, 1799 - Deed of Release - April 26, 1799 - recorded:Worlick Westwood, Jr.

464 - **Miles King / James Boyce of Norfolk** - November 29, 1798 - Indenture: Mortgage for slaves: Peter Goodwin, Dan, Jubiter, Phebe, Jerry as well as livestock. Wit: William A. Bayley, William Armistead Bayley. April 26, 1799 - recorded:Worlick Westwood, Jr.

Elizabeth City County, Virginia 1787-1800

464-465 - **Miles King / Pascow Herbert** - November 29, 1798 - Indenture for slaves and livestock: Peter Bean, Dick, Old Jubiter, Cesar, one half of Jack the blacksmith, Hannah, George, Jill and child, Old Fanny, Rose, Daniel. All part of Barbara Jones' estate. April 26, 1799 - recorded:Worlick Westwood, Jr.

465 - **John Poole / Miles King** - September 10, 1798 - Indenture for land on the Hampton River adjoining Richard Williams, Roe Cowper and John Page. Wit: Worlick Westwood, Jr., Charles King, George Cowper, Anthony Armistead. April 26, 1799 - recorded:Worlick Westwood, Jr.

466 - **Abraham Cowper / Miles King** - October 5, 1799 - Indenture for household goods, house, livestock as security for loan. Wit: W. Armistead, John Smith, Worlick Westwood, Jr., J. Handyman. April 26, 1799 - recorded:Worlick Westwood, Jr.

467 - **William Bland and Ann his wife of Norfolk / James Latimer** - November 28, 1798 - Indenture for 75 acres on the Chesapeake Bay adjoining the lands purchased by the said Latimore of one Poole which said lands were purchased of John Skinner. Wit: John Rogers, William Banks, William Brough. April 26, 1799 - recorded:Worlick Westwood, Jr.

468 - **Wilson Miles Cary / Kate** - March 10, 1799 - Deed of emancipation. Wit: Miles King, John Spooner. May 23, 1799 - recorded:Miles King.

468 - **Wilson Miles Cary** - Celeys, March 18, 1799 - A protest by Cary about an address from the House of Delegates. Not further explained. May 23, 1799 - recorded:Worlick Westwood, Jr.

469-471 - **John James Ward and his wife Mary Courtney / William Brough / Robert Brough** - March 6, 1799 - Indenture for lot in Town of Hampton: bound on the east by North Street, on

Elizabeth City County, Virginia 1787-1800

the west by lands belonging to the estate of Cornelius Thomas and James Manson on the north by John Banks on the south by John Rogers, John Jennings, Blovet Pastuer and the estate of Robert Buxton. Also slaves Ben and Phebe. Wit: R. Armistead, William Moore, William King, Samuel Bright, Richard Gilliam. June 27, 1799 - recorded:Worlick Westwood, Jr.

471-472 - **Alexander Joseph Alphonse, David Beauregard, Jane Charlotte Corbieres Beauregard and Miles King / Wilson C. Wallace** - June 25, 1799 - Indenture for 153 acres: Plantation known as Erroll: beginning at a stone in the center of a saw pitt and running to a cedar post N82E 57 ch from thence S7E to a pine in the edge of the woods thence in the woods S27E 88 1/2 ch to a new made corner tree which is a maple and a pine, each side of a dead standing oak thence S62 1/2E 16 ch to a small mulberry tree near an old oak stump. Thence S35W 43 1/2 chs to an old stump near the Main Road, thence S61W 5 1/4 ch to a new made corner tree being three pines thence N15W 121 chs coming out the woods to two small sycamore trees on a ditch, thence S78W 37 chs on the ditch thence N7W 20 1/2 chs along the Road and Mr. Needhams line thence through a marsh N44W 26chs thence along the River N11E 13 1/2 chs thence to the beginning running N15W 19 3/4 chs. Miles King purchased land of James Wallace who was given the land by his brother Robert Wallace. Wit: Robert Armistead, Robert Armistead, Jr., William Ham. June 27, 1799 - recorded:Worlick Westwood, Jr.

472 - **Martha Armistead** - Appraisement of estate December 14, 1798 - Household goods, livestock, crops. Appraisers: Thomas Robinson, G. Collier, Samuel Thomas. June 27, 1799 - recorded:Worlick Westwood, Jr.

473 - Robert Wallace - Appraisement of estate - January 22, 1789 - Household items, tools.

Elizabeth City County, Virginia 1787-1800

Slaves: Patcher, James, Cuffy, Sam, Jack the blacksmith, Bridget, Rose, Murria, Fillis and child, Sary, Nanny, Will, Dolly, Mary, Chelsey Appraisers: William Latimer, George Latimer, Joseph Cooper. June 27, 1799 - recorded:Worlick Westwood, Jr.

474 - **Robert Wallace** - Account of sale of estate - January 26, 1789 - Miles King, William Bland, James Cooper, Robert Brough, James Williams, Worlick Westwood, John Phillips, Thomas Minson, John Rogers, William Sandy, Ocarious Nettles, Randolph Roper, John Skinner, Starkey Robinson. June 27, 1799 - recorded: Worlick Westwood, Jr.

475 - **Robert Marrow, administrator of Robert Smelt / Wm. Ap. Thos. Parsons** - July 23, 1799 Indenture for 150 acres: bound on the north by lands of Michael King, on the west by the said Parsons, on the south by Johnson Tabb, deceased, on the east by Broad Creek. July 26, 1799 - recorded:Worlick Westwood, Jr.

476 - **Wm. Ap. Thos. Parsons / Robert Marrow** - July 24, 1799 - Indenture for 150 acres: See previous indenture of description. July 26, 1799 - recorded:Worlick Westwood, Jr.

477 - **Baldwin Shephard Morris** - Will - June 3, 1799 - Ann Morris, wife; Mary Bridgford, daughter mentioned. Wit: John Dewbree, Daniel Webb. July 26, 1799 - recorded.

477 - **James Latimer / Sam** - July 24, 1799 - Deed of emancipation. July 26, 1799 - recorded :Worlick Westwood, Jr.

478 - **Thomas Jiggetts** - Account of John Gimmell April 25, 1797 - John Crandol, Richard Jones, William Gimmell, Samuel Dunn, Elizabeth Jiggetts, Polly Jiggetts, Richard Young. Examiners: Ro. Shield, William Garrow, Thomas Robinson. July 26, 1799 - recorded:Worlick

Elizabeth City County, Virginia   1787-1800

Westwood, Jr.

479 - **Ann Bland** - Acknowledgement of sale - December 26, 1798 - Wit: Samuel Selden, William Vaughan. July 26, 1799 - recorded:Worlick Westwood, Jr.

480 - **William Green and Susana his wife / Richard Paine** - July 25, 1799 - Indenture for land on Hampton River: bound beginning at the river on the line between Roe Cowper and Green, thence on the River 93 feet nine inches in front, thence on said Green's land to a sycamore and from thence down the said Cowper and Green line to the river forming a triangle. Wit: George Wray, John Harper, John Brown. July 26, 1799 - recorded:Worlick Westwood, Jr.

481-482 - **Robert Sandefer Russell** - Will - November 5, 1798 - Mary Saunders, housekeeper; Penuel Russell, Peter Garrow, Francis Garrow, Richard Morris, undefined relatives; Edward Robinson, George Purdie, Jr. mentioned Slaves: Jem, Ben, Old Sarah, Hannah, Diasy, Land lying on the north and south sides of the road to Warwick. Wit: Thomas Robinson, William Allen, John Weymouth. Codicil: William Allen who lives near Thompin's Ordinary. July 26, 1799 - recorded:Worlick Westwood, Jr.

483 - **Samuel Selden and Susannah his wife / William Stores** - July 20, 1799 - Indenture for 2 pieces of land containing 29 3/4 acres total: Beginning at the Main Road near a small marked white oak tree running S43.30E 88 poles by a line of marked trees which divides the same from William Armistead's lands to the head of Hampton Creek, thence down said creek S22W 63 1/2 poles to the mouth of a gut thence up the said gut N41.30W 24 poles thence up the middle of the North branch of said gut N3W 30 perches thence N28W 14 perches thence N3W 27 1/2 perches to a gum now made a corner tree in said branch thence leaving the branch N33.75W 34

Elizabeth City County, Virginia 1787-1800

perches by a small persimmon tree, now a marked tree made to the Main Road thence the road N48E 12 perches to the beginning. Second piece: beginning at a pine by William Armistead's ditch bearing N58E from the beginning of the first parcel and distance about 28 perches, running thence N40E 57 poles to a large white oak stump thence S61W 26 perches to a gum, thence S80W 24 perches to a large dead white oak tree and a small gum, thence S18E a right line to the beginning. July 26, 1799 - recorded :Worlick Westwood, Jr.

484-485 - **William Allen and Judith his wife / William Amory of Warwick** - July 3, 1799 - Indenture for 100 acres: Bound by the land of William Williams eastwardly, by the lands of Thomas B. Armistead and Robert Many, deceased southwardly, and by a new made line of marked trees which divides the said premises from the land of Samuel Thomas westwardly and northwardly. Diagram of platt included. Wit: Michael King. July 26, 1799 - recorded: Worlick Westwood, Jr.

486-487 - **William Armistead the elder** - Will - August 23, 1799 - William Armistead the younger, Robert Armistead, Moss Armistead, sons; Euphan Graves, Rebecca Armistead, Sarah Armistead, Mary Armistead, daughters; Robinson, daughter; Richard Cary. Slaves: Africa, Bob, Priscilla, Peggy, London, Isaac, Grace, Nancy. Plantation called Bakers which was purchased of Miles King. Plantation of 450 acres. Plantation of 225 acres at the head of the Hampton River. Wit: Worlick Westwood, Samuel Selden, James Davis, Samuel Cook. September 26, 1799 - recorded:Worlick Westwood, Jr.

487 - **John Wood** - Will - January 30, 1799 - Hannah Wood, wife; Bennet Wood, Martha Wood, Robert Wood, James Wood, William Wood, children. Wit: Jno. Drewry, Sally Wilson. September 26, 1799 - recorded:Worlick Westwood,

Elizabeth City County, Virginia 1787-1800

Jr.

488 - **Michael King / Augustine Moore, Jr. / Anne King, daughter of Michael** - April 15, 1799 Indenture for slaves: Peg, Cesar, George, Venus, Lucy, Nelly, Disey and livestock to be held in trust. Wit: Roscow Parsons, John Randle, Jr. September 26, 1799 - recorded: Worlick Westwood, Jr.

489 - **Robert Brough / Ellison Skinner** - August 17, 1799 - Release of debt: paid by David Parish, husband of Rebecca, Ellison Skinner's daughter. September 26, 1799 - recorded:Worlick Westwood, Jr.

489-490 - **Robert Bright** - Accounting of estate John Seymour, Samuel Watts, John Sheppard, Mrs. Brough Bartlett, William Brough, Miles King, John Carter, James Marshall, Doctor Selden, John Robinson, Molly Carter, Charles Jennings, William Latimer, Richard Jarvis, Doctor Williams, George Booker, Augustine Moore, John Hunter, Benjamin Wooten, James Baker, George Latimer, John Kirby, Westwood Armistead, Doctor Bartlett, Josiah Massenburg, Mary Bright. Slaves: Ruth, Will, David, Fanny. Wit: Joseph Needham, Thomas Watts, Samuel Selden. September 26, 1799 - recorded:Worlick Westwood, Jr.

491 - **Jno. Parsons** - Accounting of estate, Wm. Ap. T. Parsons, Exec. - Robert Brough, Col. Westwood, John Ambler, Rev. William Bland, Matt. Anderson, James Naylor Cooper, Miles King, John Cary, Jacob Wray, Thomas Payne. Slaves: Pegg and child, Silvia and child, Phillis and two children. Wit: George Booker, Wm. Lowry, John Randle. September 26, 1799 - recorded:Worlick Westwood, Jr.

492 - **William Langhorne, Exc. of William Langhorne, Sr. who was Exc. of Wilson Curle and Lockey Curle, widow of Wilson / John Wellings** -

Elizabeth City County, Virginia 1787-1800

March 18, 1799 - Indenture for fifty acres known as Scones Dam Tract: beginning at a small marked hickory standing on the line of John Stith Westwood thence running northerly to the waters of Capt. Wm. Armistead's mill pond thence by the mill pond to an elm corner now made thence from that said pond by a line of marked trees southerly to a small gum now made a corner, thence by a line of marked trees to the beginning. Wit: William Garrow, Jno. Drewry, Maurice Langhorne, James Smelt. September 26, 1799 - recorded:Worlick Westwood, Jr.

493 - **Thomas Wooten, Jr. / Miles King** - February 23, 1782 - Bond for debt. Slave Pompey mentioned. Wit: Worlick Westwood. September 26, 1799 - recorded:Worlick Westwood, Jr.

493 - **Samuel Cunningham and his wife Sarah** - October 24, 1798 - Setting of dower of Sarah as widow of John Weymouth. Land: beginning at the 3rd row of apple trees on the north side of the orchard, running southerly to a white gum at the edge of the swamp, thence easterly to a black gum at the edge of the woods and so on to the back line joining Col. Wilson M. Cary's land. House: first room in dwelling, 1/3 kitchen, first room in barn. Wit: William Smith, John Minson, Richard H. Smith. October ___, 1799 - recorded:Worlick Westwood, Jr.

494-495 - **Thomas Jones, Jr. and his wife Sarah / John L. Westwood** - July 16, 1799 - Indenture for house and lot in Town of Hampton: bound on the north and west side by the estate of the late Francis Riddlehurst, on the south by the Hampton River and on the east by King street. Acknowledgement of Sarah to sell. Wit: Worlick Westwood and Samuel Selden. October 24, 1799 - recorded:Worlick Westwood, Jr.

495 - **Wm. Roe Cunningham and Sarah his wife /**

Elizabeth City County, Virginia 1787-1800

Thomas Skinner - October 24, 1799 - Indenture for 10 acres: bound on Mill Creek and the land of Joseph Selden. October 24, 1799 - recorded: Worlick Westwood, Jr.

496 - **John Hardyman / Wilson Miles Cary** - June 22, 1799 - Bill of Sale: household goods. October 24, 1799 - recorded:Worlick Westwood, Jr.

496 - **Archilus Yancey** - Sales of estate February 3, 1795 - William Latimer, Sr., William Latimer, Jr., Doctor J. Ward, Mrs. Maniss, Robert K. Brown, George Wray, Samuel Selden, William King, John Skinner, Miles King, Mr. Corbieres, Thomas Cain, Benjamin Rudd, William Brough, Chester Morriss, Charles Jones, Thomas Fenn, William Pierce, Edward Rudd. October 24, 1799 - recorded:Worlick Westwood, Jr.

497 - **George Booker and Ann his wife / Thomas Fenn** - October 3, 1799 - Indenture for 150 acres: lands lying on Harris Creek that formerly belonged to Capt. Samuel Curle, deceased; one half of lands lying in Sawyer Swamp formerly the maiden property of Mary Curle, deceased purchased of Thomas Fenn and Mary Baker his wife. October 24, 1799 - recorded:Worlick Westwood, Jr.

498 - **Thomas Fenn and Mary Baker his wife / George Booker** - October 22, 1799 - Indenture for 150 acres as described in the last deed Wit: James Howell, John Cooper, James Davis, Samuel Smith, John Skinner, Jno. Nicholson. October 24, 1799 - recorded:Worlick Westwood, Jr.

499 - **James Banks** - Appraisement of estate - October 5, 1795 - Household items, one boat. Wit: Thos. C. Amory, John Skinner, John Minson. October 24, 1799 - recorded:Worlick Westwood, Jr.

Elizabeth City County, Virginia 1787-1800

500 - **James Banks** - Account of sales of estate - Richard Rowland, James Burke, Wilson Wallace, John Banks, James Banks, Jno. Banks, William Westwood (purchased boat and rigging). October 1799 - recorded:Worlick Westwood, Jr.

501 - **Francis Mallory / William Mallory** - August 15, 1799 - Indenture for 12 1/2 acres: beginning at the road running S60E 94 poles thence N2 30 poles N 33 poles thence N65W 49 poles to a willow thence down the meanders of the branch to the road thence S25W 8 1/2 poles. Wit: George Booker, Samuel Cooke, Charles M. Collier, Anthony Armistead, John Chisman. October 24, 1799 - recorded:Worlick Westwood, Jr.

502 - **Patrick Walker / Robert Armistead** - October 22, 1799 - Indenture for 1/4 of a water grist mill lying in the counties of York and Elizabeth City and known by the name of Read's Mill. October 24, 1799 - recorded:Worlick Westwood, Jr.

503 - **Robert Armistead / William Armistead** - October __, 1799 - Indenture for tract of land at the head of Hampton River plus 40 acres adjoining the said tract. Part of land was inherited from parents who had purchased part from Phillip Cowper. Wit: W. Armistead, Richard H. Smith, James Parsons, Wilson C. Wallace. October 24, 1799 - recorded:Worlick Westwood, Jr.

504 - **Thomas Fenn** - Account of sales of estate - December 30, 1788 - George Latimer, John Sheppard, Thomas Fenn, William Pierce, Charles Stores, William Latimer, Archelus Yancy, John Rogers, Martha Fenn, Miles King, Arthur Henderson, Robert Brough. October 24, 1799 - recorded:Worlick Westwood, Jr.

505 - **Robert Smelt** - Appraisement of estate - October 19, 1796 - Household items, tools

Elizabeth City County, Virginia 1787-1800

Slaves: Colley, Tom, Joe, Nanny, Patty, Tom, George. Appraisers: Wm. A.T. Parsons, Michael King, Henry Tabb. October 24 - recorded: Worlick Westwood, Jr.

506-507 - **Robert Smelt** - Accounts of estate, Robert Marrow, Admin. - Miles King, Dr. Applewhaite, Mrs. Tompkins, Henry Tabb, Jno. Sanders, James Davis, James Smelt, Dr. Ward, Major Parsons, Mrs. Wray, Mrs. Robert Armistead, William Allen, Miles Smelt, David Smelt, Richard Cary. Slaves: Tom, Colley, Nancy, Joe, Patty, Isom, George. October 1799 - recorded:Worlick Westwood, Jr.

507 - **Archilus Yancey** - Accounting of estate, William Pierce, Admin. - Subscribers: M. King, A. Henderson, Merritt Moore, David Yancey, Charles Yancey, Jno. Nicholson, Jno. Shepard, Wm. King. October 24, 1799 - recorded:Worlick Westwood, Jr.

508 - **Robet Landrum** - Appraisement of estate - January 26, 1796 - Furniture and bedding. Appraisers: Wm. A. Parsons, Michael King, Robert Marrow, Wm. Armistead. Account of sales: William Landrum, John Willings, Merritt Moore, Miles King, John Wellings, Jno. Drewry, C. Bayley, John Skinner. Examiners: Michael King, William Armistead, Robert Marrow. October 24, 1799 - recorded:Worlick Westwood, Jr.

509 - **Mrs. Bell (Margaret)** - Sales of estate - October 4, 1798 - Alexander Maney, Miss Giney Bell, James Bell, Nathaniel Bell, Samuel Thomas, William Allen, James Halaway, John Yeargain, Robert Armistead, Robert Sandefur, John Skinner. October 24, 1799 - recorded: Worlick Westwood, Jr.

510 - **Margaret Bell** - Accounts of estate, William Allen, Admin. - John L. Westwood, Mrs. Weymouth, Robert Sandefur, David Spruce.

Elizabeth City County, Virginia 1787-1800

Examiners: Michale King, Thomas Robinson, Charles M. Collier. October 24, 1799 - recorded:Worlick Westwood, Jr.

511 - **Miles King / William Roe Cunningham** - November 21, 1799 - Deed of Release for 10 acres. December 26, 1799 - recorded:Worlick Westwood, Jr.

512 - **Peter Fiveash (late of the County of Norfolk but presently of Elizabeth City County)** - Will - July 30, 1799 - Captain John Tabb, William Latimer mentioned. Wife and children mentioned by not named. Wit: John Shepard, Laurence Haynes, Richard Routen. January 23, 1799 - recorded:Worlick Westwood, Jr.

513 - **Thomas Skinner / Levi Thomas** - December 26, 1799 - Indenture for 40 acres: bound by the lands of James Latimer and Abraham Pickett. Land was inherited by Skinner from his father. December 26, 1799 - recorded: Worlick Westwood, Jr.

514 - **Mark Hall** - Appraisement of estate - April 1796 - Household goods. Slaves: Frank, Nan. Appraisers: James N. Cooper, Thomas Minson. January 23, 1800 - recorded:Worlick Westwood, Jr.

515-519 - **Robert Smelt** - Account of sales of estate - October 20, 1796 - John Yeargain, William Landrum, Robert Marrow, John Skinner, Sr., Worlick Westwood, Miles King, William Presson, Jno. Drewry, Sr., James Davis, Jno. Landrum, Wm. Smelt, William Allen, James Cunningham, Penuel Sands, Augustine Moore, Sr., Wm. A.T.Parsons, David Smelt, Jr. James Burke, John Wood, Samuel Cunningham, John Russell, David Smelt, Bartlet Field, James Saunders, Robert Lowry, John Willings, Westwood Armistead, Henry Tabb, Mrs. Tompkins, Michael King, Cinthia Smelt. Slaves: Joe, Tom, Colley, Patty, Nancy, Old Dick, George. January 23,

Elizabeth City County, Virginia 1787-1800

1800 - recorded:Worlick Westwood, Jr.

519-520 - **Jacob Wray** - Will - February 2, 1797 - George Wray, John Ashton Wray, sons; Mary Ann Wray, Elizabeth Stuart, Helen Wray Stuart, Nancy Wray Stuart, granddaughters; Jacob Wray Stuart, grandson; John A. Stuart, son-in-law (?); Charles Stuart, son-in-law. Slaves: Jenny and children, Milla, John, Grace. Wit: George Booker, Thomas Jones, John L. Westwood. Codicil: November 29, 1798 - Gives entire estate to George Wray. John Ashton Wray has died. February 27, 1800 - recorded:Worlick Westwoo, Jr.

521 - **John Curle King** - Will - January 20, 1800 - Elizabeth King, wife; John Curle King the younger, son; Hannah Herbert King, daughter; Samuel Watts mentioned. Slave: Will. Wit: Pascow Herbert, Mary Herbert, William King. February 27, 1800 - recorded:Worlick Westwood, Jr.

522 - **James Berry** - Will - February 7, 1800 - Ann Berry, wife; James Berry the younger, son; Elizabeth Davis mentioned. Wit: R. Armistead, John Wilson. February 27, 1800 - recorded: Worlick Westwood, Jr.

522-523 - **John Skinner** - Will - November 21, 1799 - Mrs. Lively mentioned; John Skinner the younger, son; other children mentioned but not named; George Booker mentioned. Wit: A.P. Dessenis, Thomas P. Roberts, Rebecah Russell. February 1800 - recorded:Worlick Westwood, Jr.

524 - **Sarah Cunningham** - Acknowledgement of sale of land - January 13, 1800 - Wit: William Brough, Samuel Selden. February 27, 1800 - recorded:Worlick Westwood, Jr.

525 - **William Brough / Robert Brough of Norfolk** - August 1, 1799 - Bill of sale for slaves: Hampton Manuel, Lancaster, George, Jenny,

Elizabeth City County, Virginia 1787-1800

Phillis, Venus and her child Sam, Sylvia and her child Billy, Rachael, Hannah, Beck, Anthony, Patience, Jack. Also livestock, household goods. Sale to be void if money paid back. Wit: Corbin Spriggy, Mark Parish. February 27, 1800 - recorded:Worlick Weswood, Jr.

526 - **Captain Joseph Meredith** - Account of estate, Elizabeth Meredith, Exec. - September 25, 1799 - Miles King, David Brodie, Job Parker, William Lattermore, Jno. L. Westwood, William Pennock, George Hope, John J. Spooner, Doctor Applewhaite. Examiners: W. E. Chisman, Wm. Kerby, Jno. L. Westwood, George Wray. February 27, 1800 - recorded:Worlick Westwood, Jr.

527 - **Martha Armistead** - Account of estate, Wm. Allen, Exec. - January 23, 1800 - Miles King. Examiners: R. Armistead, ___. Armistead, William Allen. February 27, 1800 - recorded:Worlick Westwood, Jr.

528-529 - **Robert Wallace** - Account of estate, Worlick Westwood, Exec. - William Pierce, William Bland, R. Armistead, John Cooper, George Latimer, Miles King, Doctor Colton, William Sandy, Capt. Rogers, William Brough, Pascow Herbert, John Perry, Johnson Tabb, Mark Hall, Doctor Applewhaite, Ocarious Nettles, Richard Hackney, Major Fenn, William King, Thomas Fenn, Samuel Selden, Mrs. McClurg, Peter Tinsley, Richard Cary, Doctor Hamm. Slaves: Cuff, Sam, Bridget, Nan, Portshire, Rose, Jack, Sarah, Dolly, Mary. Examiners: W.E. Chisman, Jno. L. Westwood, Charles Jennings. February 27, 1800 - recorded:Worlick Westwood, Jr.

530 - **David Saunders** - Account of estate, William Saunders, Admin. - January 27, 1800 - William Seymour, Francis Ross, Jr., William Parsons, John Sanders, Samuel Cook, William

Elizabeth City County, Virginia 1787-1800

Allen, John Dewbry, John Skinner, Ann Sanders, Robert Sanderfur Russell. Examiners: R. Armistead, W. Armistead, William Allen. February 27, 1800 - recorded:Worlick Westwood, Jr.

531-532 - **Commonwealth of Virginia / Sheriff of Elizabeth City County** - Writ of Quod Damnum - Request of George Purdie to build a tidewater grist mill on his land lying on one side of the North Branch of Back River in the County of York. Heirs of David Blaney mentioned. Jury: George Wray, Thomas Jones, John Cooper, William Allen, William Armistead, John Skinner, John Shepard, Simon Hollier, Samuel Bright, James Parsons, Thomas Fenn, Henry Tabb.

Commonwealth of Virginia / Sheriff of York County - Summons for Mrs. Mallory, Mary Sclater, John Robinson, Arron Tennis to testify to the permit of George Purdie to build a dam. Only John Robinson opposed the dam although he admits it will not much effect his property.

Elizabeth City County, Virginia 1787-1800

Elizabeth City County, Virginia 1787-1800

ELIZABETH CITY COUNTY

DEED BOOK 34

This is an All Name index of persons. Negroes are listed together alphabetally under the heading "Negroes." Page numbers refer to the actual page of the document as it appears in the deed book. Numbers in bold indicate wills, or major activity of the person listed.

Allen, Bethia 204
Allen, Betsy 98, **247**
Allen, Edward 98, **330**
Allen, Edwards 15a
Allen, Elizabeth **330**
Allen, Henry 61, 306
Allen, Hudson 123
Allen, John 9, 23, 101, 240, 291, 342, 377, 410, 417, **420,** 446
Allen, Judith **484**
Allen, Thomas 7, 21, 36, 61, 128, 211, 253, 255, 292, **386**, 436
Allen, William 23, 100, 132, 134, 155, 161, 240, **249**, 252, 289, 307, 362, **366**, 377, 421, 436, 440, **449**, 456, 481, **484**, 506, 509, **510**, 515, **527,** 530, 531
Allen, William Jr. 377
Allen, William Sr. 227, 292
Allyne, Samuel 201
Ambler, Jacquilen (Treasurer of Virginia) 3, 227
Ambler, John 491
Amory, Thomas C. 206, 499
Amory, William (of Warwick) **484**
Anderson, Matt 491
Andrews, Robert 182 (Math Professor, William & Mary)
Applewhaite, Doctor 7, 14, 100, 255, 362, 417, 506, 527, 528
Applewhaite, John 56, **58,** 78, **112,** 201, 214, 255, 296, **372**, 400
Applewhaite, Jno. 353, 436
Archer, Abraham 227

Elizabeth City County, Virginia 1787-1800

Archer, Edward   185
Archer, Thomas   227
Armistead, ____ Mrs.   253, 255
Armistead, Ann   **111**, 185, 380, **454**
Armistead, Anthony   **16** (of North Carolina), 190, 465, 507
Armistead, Catherine   **126**
Armistead, Edward   249
Armistead, Elizabeth   **111**, **358**, 377
Armistead, Euphan   **150**
Armistead, Francis   **358**
Armistead, Francis Mennis   **449**
Armistead, Gile   **19, 247**
Armistead, Hannah   **247**
Armistead, James B.   **30, 78**, 227
Armistead, James Bray   **19, 20**, 31
Armistead, John   31, **36**, 227
Armistead, Martha   249, 341, **449, 472, 527**
Armistead, Martha Tompkins   **449**
Armistead, Mary   16, **151**, 201, **486**
Armistead, Moses   **79, 84, 86**
Armistead, Mosley   190, 330
Armistead, Moss   227, **248**, **380, 486**
Armistead, Nancy   380
Armistead, Polly   380
Armistead, Priscilla   380
Armistead, R.   64, 331, 366, 389, 420, 455, 469, 522, 527, 528, 530
Armistead, Rebecca   **486**
Armistead, Robert   1, 7, **15a**, 24, **26**, 50, 52, **61, 63**, 96, 98, 100, 111, **169, 173**, 175, **182**, 201, 227, **249, 253, 255**, 292, 317, **318**, 319, **322**, 327, 330, 341, **356**, 362, 368, **377**, 386, 391, **392, 392**, 417, 427, **436, 439**, 471, **486, 502, 503**, 506, 509
Armistead, Robert Jr.   **318**, 471
Armistead, Robert Sr.   **111**
Armistead, Robinson (daughter of William)   486
Armistead, Samuel   **449**
Armistead, Sarah   **150, 486**
Armistead, Sedwell   177
Armistead, Thomas B.   30, 78, 111, 128, 142, 167, 253, 255, 286, 287, 319, 373, 374, 377, 456, 484

Elizabeth City County, Virginia 1787-1800

Armistead, Thomas Baker **451, 454**
Armistead, W. 466, 503, 530
Armistead, Westwood **21, 24,** 227, 330, 446, 489, 515
Armistead, William 7, 11, 28, 61, **63, 84, 111,** 131, 132, **147, 150, 151, 151,** 175, 190, 206, **249,** 267, 282, **321,** 327, 330, 338, **358,** 360, 369, 376, **380,** 412, 415, 439, 460, 483, 492, **503,** 508, 531
Armistead, William (Capt.) **19,** 255
Armistead, William Jr. 24, **190,** 253, **420, 486** (the younger)
Armistead, William Sr. 138, **415,** 420, **486** (the elder)
Armisteade, Elizabeth **1**
Armisteade, John **1**
Armisteade, Robert **1**
Backhouse, Richard **197, 428, 429**
Badget, William 211
Badgitt, William **324**
Bailey, Ann 161
Bailey, Deana Wallace **167**
Bailey, William 227
Bailey, William Armistead (of Norfolk) **161,** 162
Baines, Fanny 410
Baines, John 240
Baines, Matthew 223, **410**
    Also see: Bains, Banes
Bains, Fanny 360
Bains, George 66
Bains, John 55, **207,** 223, 342, 377
Bains, Samuel 66
    Also see: Baines, Banes
Baker, __ 164
Baker, James 56, 62, **132, 327,** 452, 489
Baker, Rebecca **297, 327**
Baker, Timothy 406
Ballard, Edward 42, 63, 403, **441** (Capt.), **463**
Ballard, Francis 189, 201, **463**
Ballard, Fras. 71
Ballard, James 98, 352
Ballard, James S. **463**
Ballard, John **297**

Elizabeth City County, Virginia 1787-1800

Ballard, Sarah **463**
Ballard, Servant 46, 62, 66, 112, 113, **297**, 423, 436
Banes, Henry **410**
Banes, John 291, 292, **410**
Banes, Mary **455**
Banes, Matthew **455**
Banes, Richard **410**
Banes, William **410**
    Also see: Baines, Bains
Banks, J. 406
Banks, Jas. 138
Banks, James 189, 235, 270, 293, **499**, **500**, 500
Banks, James Jr. 243
Banks, John 121, **130**, 138, 169, 173, 185, 211, **211**, 214, 218, 235, 302, 352, 359, 363, 469, 500
Banks, John Jr. 235, 243, **348**
Banks, John Sr. **348**
Banks, Jno. 37, 82, 113, 138, 293, 356, 411, 436, 500
Banks, Mary **211**
Banks, William 313, 467
Barbary, Mary Ann **238**
Barnaba, Richard 360
Barnes, Aron 101
Barraclough, John 148, 170
Barron, ____ 438
Barron, Elizabeth **201**, **400**
Barron, Elizabeth Mosley **201**
Barron, James 43, 56, **65**, 133, **201**
Barron, Jane **133**
Barron, Rebecca **18**
Barron, Richard **18**, 56, 352, 427
Barron, Samuel **57**, **65**, 109, 133, **201**, **400**
Barron, Sarah 441
Bartlett, ____(Dr.) 489
Bartlett, Brough, Mrs. 489
Bast, Richard 452
Bates, George **243**, 280, 315, **388**
Bayley, ____ 337
Bayley, ___ (Mrs.) 7
Bayley, C. 508
Bayley, Charles **58**, 139, **177**, **297**

Elizabeth City County, Virginia 1787-1800

Bayley, Diane W. 78
Bayley, Diane Wallace **19**, **64**
Bayley, Elizabeth Wallace **64**
Bayley, Frances **177**, **297**
Bayley, J. W. 227
Bayley, James 142, **285**, 286, **373**, **411**, 436
Bayley, John 285, **286**, 287, 330, **374**
Bayley, Thomas **11**, 72, 123, 159, **177**, **297**, 336
Bayley, Walter 142, 285, 286
Bayley, William **177**, **297**, 302, 360, **393**
Bayley, William A. **411**, 464
Bayley, William Armistead **189**, 285, 464
Bayley, Wilson Wallace **19**, **64**
Bayly, Nicholas 16
Bean, Elizabeth 383
Bean, John 46
Beane, John 275
Beauregard, Alexander Joseph Alphonse David **460**, **471**
Beauregard, Jane Charlotte Corbieres **471**
Bedingford, Mary **406**
Bedingfield, Nathaniel **400**, **406**
Bedingfield, W. 392
Been, Charles 360
Been, Elizabeth **20**
Been, James **20**
Been, John **20**, 114, 300, **355**, 359, 360, 392, 409
Been, Jno. 392, 436
Been, Martha **20**
Belfour, James 139
Bell, ___ (Mrs.) 362
Bell, Giney 509
Bell, James 456, 509
Bell, Jane 100
Bell, John 100
Bell, Margaret 449, **509**, **510**
Bell, Mary **449**
Bell, Nathaniel **100**, 101, 509
Bell, Natt 9, 101
Bennett, ___ 414 (orphan)
Bennett, John **137**, 141
Bennett, William 12, **406** (of Surry)
Berry, _____ (Mrs.) 23

121

Elizabeth City County, Virginia 1787-1800

Berry, Ann **522**
Berry, James 206, **522**
Black, Mary 226
Black, Peter 360
Blacke, Ba 202
Bland, Ann **467, 479**
Bland, Samuel 234, **390**
Bland, William (Rev.) **87, 467** (of Norfolk), 474, 491, 528
Blane, Thomas (of London) **263**
Blaney, David 531
Blaxton, _____ (Mrs.) 23
Booker, ___ (Mr.) 29, 101, 141
Booker, Ann 246, **297**
Booker, G. 442
Booker, George 1, 7, **41**, 43, 72, 84 123, 124, **127, 128**, 155, **160**, 162, 189, 201, 211, 220, 227, **237**, 246, **253**, 255, 272, 273, 285, 286, 287, 291, 309, **319**, 333, 345, 359, 360, 362, 369, 380, 391, 420, 436, 489, 491, **497, 498**, 501, 506, 519, 523
Borrowdale, Ann 198
Borrowdale, Anne Rosetta **198, 302**
Borrowdale, James **170**, 175, **178, 198**, 302, 445
Boush, Charles L. (of Norfolk) **375**
Boush, Prudence **375** (of Norfolk)
Boush, Robert 375
Boutwell, Ann **131, 226**, 462
Bowery, Grace Elizabeth **60, 62, 93, 183**
Bowery, Mary Courtney **60, 93, 184, 185, 217, 218**
Bowrey, Robert **93**
Bowry, Eleanor **308**
Boyce, James **161, 189**, 464 (of Norfolk)
Boyce, Joe 375
Boyd, ___ 201
Bracken, John 182 (Humanities Professor, William and Mary)
Brent, Thomas 185
Bridgford, Mary **477**
Bright, Francis **365**
Bright, Francis Riddlehurst **311**
Bright, John 155, 166, 179, 188, 234, 235, 249, 252, 269, 279, 280, 285, **305, 311,**

Elizabeth City County, Virginia 1787-1800

   319, 323, 330, 331, 335, 336, 337, 345,
      364, **365**, 393, 414, 489
Bright, Mary **311, 409**, 489
Bright, Robert **311, 498**
Bright, Samuel 81, **365**, 460, 469, 531
Britian (Brittian), John 302, 389, 406, 441
Brodie, David 41, 99, **127, 128**, 189, 194, 243,
      313, 345, 526
Brodie, John 31 (Dr.), 227, 313 (Dr.)
Brooke, Robert (Governor of Virginia) **322**
Brough, Amelia 288
Brough, Elizabeth **185**
Brough, Grace 42
Brough, James 424
Brough, Rob 29, 60, 62, 69, 183
Brough, Robert 7, **14, 24**, 31, 34, **41**, 42, 43,
    45, 49, 93, 100, 101, 106, 109, **110, 184**,
    185, 211, **217, 218**, 253, **280**, 288, 318,
    324, **333, 334**, 345, 363, 380, **384, 419,**
    423, 436, **469**, 474, **489**, 491, 504, **525**
Brough, William 12, 33, **42**, 60, **63**, 86, 93,
    106, 143, 144, 155, **184**, 185, 194, 216,
    217, **253**, 258, **280, 281, 318**, 319, 326,
    333, 334, 339, 359, 360, 363, 364, 431,
    432, 438, 444, 445, 446, 467, **469**, 489,
    496, 524, **525**, 528
Brown, _____ (Mr.) 29
Brown, John 29, 480
Brown, Richard 227
Brown, Robert 136, 159, 305
Brown, Robert K. 496
Brown, William 31, 247, 299, 360, 362
Bryan, Benjamin 4, 16, 56, 82, 95, 123, 124,
    143, 144, 145, 175, 190, 194, 251, 308,
    353
Bryan, Mary **353**
Bryan, Patsy **353**
Bryan, William 14, 54, **353**
Buck, Benjamin 292
Bullock, James 20, 194
Bullock, Mary 20, 194
Bullock, Thomas Webster 338
Bully (Bulley), Andrew 119, 122, 157, 336, 403
Bully, Edward 360

Elizabeth City County, Virginia 1787-1800

Bully, Thomas 158, 159, 360
Burgess, William 221
Burke (Burk), James **16**, 37, 58, 68, **99**, 109, 245, **269**, 366, 385, 436, **442**, 462, 500, 515
Burke, Robert 109
Burket, Samuel 19, 51, 255, 360
Burkette, Samuel **245**
Burnham, ___ Mr. 324
Burnham, John 227
Burt, Elizabeth 68, 284
Burt, Rebecca 68, 284
Burt, Richard **283**
Burt, Sarah **68, 283**, 284
Burwell, Nathaniel 227
Bushell, Elizabeth **159**
Bushell, John, Jr. **159**
Bushell, Joseph 28, **75**, **77**, **107**, 279, 282, 360
Bushell, William 360
Butt, Ann **311**
Butte, Thomas **311**
Buxton, Ann **309**
Buxton, Betsy 176
Buxton, Elizabeth **376**
Buxton, Robert **45**, **110**, 185, 218, 318, 469
Buxton, Robert G. 43
Buxton, Sally 176
Buxton, Sarah **376**
Cabell, William, Jr. 231
Cain, Thomas **159**, 205, 496
Carbier, Angelique Henretta Louslow Herren **164**
Carbier, Paul **168**
    ALSO SEE: CORBIER
Carlton, Mary **126**, **311**
Carter, John 489
Carter, Molly 489
Cary, ___ Col. 120
Cary, John 1, 116, **247**, 255, 380
Cary, John (Col.) 111, 125, 491
Cary, Miles 53, 57, 58, 99, 132, 145, 150, 151, 151, 191, 238, **247**, 267, 296, 319, 364, 380, 414
Cary, Nelson Miles 330
Cary, Richard 50, 52, 84, **139**, 150, 151, 151,

Elizabeth City County, Virginia 1787-1800

    191, 227, **247**, 327, 380, **486**, 506, 528
Cary, Robert   **247**
Cary, Sarah   **15**, **191** (of Warwick County), 193
Cary, Susannah   **247**
Cary, W. M.   197
Cary, William   **53**, **191**
Cary, Wilson   15
Cary, Wilson M. (Col.)   493
Cary, Wilson Miles   **15**, **66**, 110, 194, 330, 429, **443**, **468**, **468**, **496**
Casey, John   66
Chambers, Mary   56
Chapman, Elizabeth   **93**
Chapman, Richard   60, **93**
Chisman, ___   526
Chisman, John   458, 501
Chisman, M. E.   376
Chisman, Thomas   227, 387
Chisman, W. E.   526, 528
Clark, John   157, **158**
Clausell, Richard   227
Clay, Abia   31
Cleaves, Willis Wilson   436
Clurg, W.   227
Cobbs, Elizabeth   55
Cobbs, Thomas   55
Cokes, Roby   31, 324
Collier, Charles   50, 377, 449
Collier, Charles M.   131, 501, 510
Collier, Charles Miles   377
Collier, G.   472
Collier, Lackey   52, 227, 377
Colton, ___ Dr.   100, 528
Colton, Ann   42, 106, **288**, **333**, **334**
Colton, Job   42, **106**, 183, 218, **288**, 333 (Doctor)
Colton, Samuel   **288**
Conniers, Charles   359
Cook, Francis   515
Cook, James   255
Cook, Samuel   233, 486, 501, 530
Cooper, Abraham   443, 452
Cooper, George   25, 159, 202
Cooper, James   75, 385, 474

Elizabeth City County, Virginia 1787-1800

Cooper, James N.   77, 131, 134, 141, 141, 171, 176, 209, 281, 282, 287, 289, 409, 514
Cooper, James Naylor   **122**, **351**, **371**, 491
Cooper, Jane   11
Cooper, John   **128**, 148, 172, 176, 194, 209, 289, 364, **371**, **376**, 377, 390, 460, 498, 528, 531
Cooper, Joseph   11, **13**, 14, 25, 50, 52, 87, 88, 115, 123, **128**, 131, 134, 141, 141, 159, 168, **171**, 172, 176, 209, 282, 287, 309, 473
Cooper, Joseph, Jr.   161, 172, 176, 202, 234
Cooper, Roe   **10**, 43
Cooper, Susanna   176
Cooper, William   176, 462
   ALSO SEE: COWPER
Copeland, Demsey   **98**
Copeland, Nancy   **98**
Corbier, Henrietta I. A.   **209**
Corbieres, Angelque Henriette Loustead Widon Herrone   **460**
Corbieres, Mr.   496
   ALSO SEE: CARBIER
Counsel, Michael   155
Couper, Rough (Roe Cooper ?)   124
Cowper, ___ Col.   436
Cowper, Abraham   **231**, **289**, 392, 414, **466**
Cowper, Edward   **204**, 320
Cowper, George   465
Cowper, James   242
Cowper, James K.   10, 11
Cowper, James N.   253
Cowper, Jane   **11, 242**
Cowper, John   242
Cowper, Joseph   7
Cowper, Mary   155
Cowper, Phillip   10, 11, 369, 503
Cowper, Roe   4, **11**, **139**, 155, **242**, **299**, 465, 480
Cowper, Sarah   11, 242
   ALSO SEE: COOPER
Crandol, James   227
Crandol, John   478
Crandle, Richard   101, 227

Elizabeth City County, Virginia 1787-1800

Crawford, R___ C. 401
Creek, John 15
Creshy, Samuel W. 227
Crook, Penuel 211
Crosby, Minson 24
Cunningham, ___ 213, 405
Cunningham, Elizabeth **43**
Cunningham, James 37, **121**, 177, 245, 311, 350, 360, 389, 404, 412, 414, 515
Cunningham, Samuel **19**, 61, **121**, **121**, 428, 452, **493**, 515
Cunningham, Samuel Barron 43
Cunningham, Samuel R. 51
Cunningham, Sarah **493**, **494**, **524**
Cunningham, William **43**, **121**, 350
Cunningham, Wm. Roe **495**, **511**
Curle, ___ 400, 421
Curle, Elizabeth **84**
Curle, Lockey **492**
Curle, Mary **171**, 380, **430**, **440**, 497
Curle, Samuel (Capt.) 497
Curle, William Roscow Wilson **171**
Curle, Wilson 13, **84**, 294, 380, 452, **492**
Cutiller, Abraham 118
Cutiller, Edward **118**
Cutliler, Mary **118**
Cutillo, Edward 458
Daes, James **106**
Davenport, James 277
Davenport, W. 139
Davenport, William 70, 227, 238
Davis, David 173, 356
Davis, Elizabeth **223**, **226**, 522
Davis, Herbert (Capt.) 380
Davis, James **55**, 100, 206, 289, 292, **335**, 336, 337, 342, 345, 362, 377, 386, 410, 417, 436, **455**, 456, 486, 498, 506, 515
Davis, John 364, **414**
Davis, Mary **369** (of Isle of Wight County)
Davis, William 88, 246
Davis, Wilson **369** (of Isle of Wight County)

Daws, Bartholomew **338**
Daws, Ezekial **338**

Elizabeth City County, Virginia 1787-1800

Daws, Gilbert **338**
Daws, John **338**
Daws, Rachel **338**
Daws, Sarah **338**
Daws, William **338**
Dedman, B. 118
Delaney (Delany), Edward 37, **69**, 183, **309**, 404
Delaney, Elizabeth **309**
Delaney, John **309**
Delaney, Pamela **309**
Dessenis, A. P. 522
Dewberry, Mrs. 207
Dewbre, James H. **223**
Dewbre, John **55**, 335, 362, 477
Dewbre, Rebecca **55**, **240**, 342
Dewbre, Samuel 55
Dewbre, Thomas 342
Dewbre, Thomas N. **223**
Dewbre, Thomas W. 336, **337**
Dewbre, Thomas Whitby 335
    ALSO SEE: DEWBRY
Dewbry, ____ Mrs. 206
Dewbry, John **223**, 292, 342, 345, 530
Dewbry, Rebecca **223**, **342**, **345**
Dewbry, Samuel 324
Dewbry, Thomas 324, 392
Diggs, Cole 227
Diggs, Dudley 227 (Col.)
Diggs, William 84, 191, 197, 324, 429
Dixon, A. T. 428
Dixon, Anne **197** (of Charles City County), **429**
Dixon, Anthony F. **197** (of Charles City County)
Dixon, Elizabeth 359
Dixon, James 36, 190, 227, 436, 510
Dixon, Mary 359
Dixon, Richard 25, 28, 38, 39, 40, 54, 70, 75,
    81, 106, 182, **359**
Dixon, Sarah 16, 58, **83**
Dixon, Servant 428
Dixon, Thomas 66, **463**
Dobbins, William 154, 360
Dobson, Mary **305**
Dobson, Robert 302, **305**, 339, 363
Donovill, Samuel 429

Elizabeth City County, Virginia 1787-1800

Douglass, John 383
Drew, Hannah **311**
Drew, William **311**
Drewry, John 134, 161, 417, 487, 492, 508
Drewry, Jno., Sr. 515
Drewry, William 134
Dubond, J. 184, 185
Dubond, Jerome 334
Dudley, William 191
Dufour, William Joseph 308
Duke, John (of Louisa County) 224, **224**
Dunkley, John 152
Dunn, E. 227
Dunn, Henry 62
Dunn, John 101, 227
Dunn, Samuel 478
Dunn, Susannah 108
Dunn, William **211**, 463
Dunoway, Eppa 360, 362
Durant, Henry 359
Eastin, Howard 227
Elliott, Chevers **298**
Elliott, Harry **309**
Elliott, Henry 427
Elliott, Henry Howard **462**
Elliott, Martha **309**
Elliott, Robert 66, 162, 216, **309**
Elliott, Thomas **309**
Elliott, William **309**, **462**
    ALSO SEE: ELOTT
Ellis, Samuel (Capt.) **406**
Elott, Chaves **96**
Elott, Robert **96**
Everard, Mr. 227
Everard, Thomas 227
Face, Edward 13, 16, 37, 38, 39, 40, 46, 81,
    82, 130, 130, 138, 204, 211, 235, 270,
    275, **314**, **315**, 345, 352, **386**, 404, 411
Face, Frances 275
Fathercloth, William Reid 26
Fenn, Major 528
Fenn, Martha 504
Fenn, Mary Baker 497, **498**
Fenn, Thomas 87, 225, 290, 327, 390, 451, 454,

Elizabeth City County, Virginia   1787-1800

   496, **497**, **498**, **504**, 504, 528, 531
Field, Bartlet(t)   7, 30, 142, 267, 324, 374,
   436, 515
Fields, ____ Mr.   417
Fields, John   7, 15a, 276, 366
Fields, Rosea   324
Fields, Rosey   **15a**
Finnie, Joanna   **175** (of Prince George County)
Finney, Jno   185
Finney, John   184
Fiveash, Peter   **512**
Foster, Anne   **162**
Foster, Seth   **161**, **162**
Francis, Hannah   118, 458
Frazer, Elizabeth   141
Frazer, William   60, 217, 280
Freshwater, Thaddious   380
Galt, G. M.   247
Gardnor, Mary   69
Garner, Thomas   56
Garrott, Thomas   227
Garrow, Francis   **481**
Garrow, John   292
Garrow, Peter   **481**
Garrow, William   233, 478, 492
George, John   118
Gibbons, Robert   53
Gile, James   211
Gilliam, Richard   309, 469
Gimmell, John   **478**
Gimmell, William   478
Goddin, William   **349**
Godwin, William   **391**
Gooch, Elizabeth   **108**
Gooch, Polly   **108**
Gooch, Sarah   **108**
Gooch, William   5, 16, **108**, 197, 227, 283, 284,
   429
Goodwin, James   19, 100, 227
Goodwin, Peter   464
Gouge, Mathew   31
Graves, Euphan   **486**
Graves, William   404
Grayson, John   510

130

Elizabeth City County, Virginia 1787-1800

Green, Susana **480**
Green, William 242, 266, **299, 300**, 355, **480**
Greenhow, George 277
Greenhow, Robert **277** (of Williamsburg)
Griffin, ___ Dr. 227
Gunther, John 227
Gussel, Adam 7
Guy, James 436
Guy, William 65, 81, 166, 184, 185, 241, 266, 360

Hackeny, Richard 528
Hains, Larrance **453**
Hains, Patsy **453**
Hains, Samuel **453**
Hains, Susana **453**
Halaway, James 407, 509
    ALSO SEE: HALLOWAY, HOLLOWAY
Hall, David 140
Hall, Mark 10, 75, 77, 114, 119, 136, **140, 514**, 528
Hall, T. 152
Halloway, Robert 436
    ALSO SEE: HALAWAY, HOLLOWAY
Hamm, ___ Doctor 7, 528
Hamm, Valentine, Dr. 324
Hamm (Hame, Ham) William 405, 471
Hanbury, Capel 248
Hanbury, Osgood 248
Handyman, J. 466
Hannasin, James 14
Hansford, Charles 227
Hardiman, J. 311
Hardyman, John **406, 496**
Harper, Charity 39, **130, 424**
Harper, John **13, 38, 39, 40**, 81, 82, **130**, 132, 138, 235, 302 (Jr.), 305, 348, 358, 363, 412, 480
Harper, William **302**
Harris, John (Capt.) **144**
Harwood, Humphrey **458**
Harwood, Martha **458**
Hatton, Thomas 16, 29, **58, 66**, 113, 121, 122, 211, 255

131

Elizabeth City County, Virginia   1787-1800

Haughton, Robert (of Warwick County)   123
   ALSO SEE: Houghton
Hawkins, Anthony   197, 429, 452
Hayes, John   227
Hayes, Jno.   100
Haynes, ___ Doctor   101
Haynes, Anne   **152**
Haynes, Laurence   512
Haynes, Susanah   **409**
Haynes, Thomas   227
Healy, Samuel   177, 297
Henderson, A.   507
Henderson, Ann   **226**
Henderson, Arthur   14, **54**, 123, **216**, **226**, 304, 336, 359, **403**, 504
Henderson, James II   182 (Humanities Professor, William and Mary)
Henderson, William   227
Herbert, ___ Capt.   18, 109, 392
Herbert, Mary   4, **34**, **49**, **214**, 521
Herbert, Pascow   4, **49**, 95, **110**, 177, 190, **214**, 293, 297, 298, **311**, 320, **326**, 436, **452**, **464**, 521, 528
Hewitt, William   227
Hicks, David   184, 185, 387
Hicks, Frankey   317
Hicks, John   38, 81, 82, 130, 275, 387
Hicks, William   45, 185, **318**, 375
Hirst, Henry   139
Hodge, William   392
Holland, Mary M.   417
Holland, William M.   **417**
Hollier, Ann   **53**
Hollier, Simon   **29**, **53**, 531
Holmes, Robert (of London)   263
Holloway, Robert   100
   ALSO SEE: HALAWAY, HALLAWAY
Hoomes, John   **216** (of Caroline County)
Hope, George   34, 37, **43**, 45, **49**, **71**, 109, 110, **113**, 143, 144, 147, 162, **190**, **191**, **201**, **202**, 202, **204**, 206, 214, 251, **266**, 302, 305, 356, 392, 405, 416, 420, 423, 431, 432, 438, 526
Hope, George, Jr.   147, 356, 358

Elizabeth City County, Virginia 1787-1800

Hope, George, Sr. 311
Hopkins, Warren 42, 43, 45, **113**, 147, 305, 423, 436
Hopson, Charles 227
Houghton, William 436
   ALSO SEE: Haughton
Howard, Henry 118, 227
Howell, James **426**, 498
Hudson, George 152
Humphlet, Edward 68
Humphlet, Elizabeth **106**, **221**, **283**, **284**
Humphlet, King 106
Humphlet, Thomas 5, 87, 100, **106**, 107, **221**, 436
Hundley, Charles 147
Hundley, Robert 147
Hunger, William J. 423
Hunt, William 14, 37, 65, 97, 113, 327
Hunter, John 31, 46, 101, 234, **238**, 489
Hunter, John Capt. 23, 339
Hunter, Susanna **214**, **238**
Hunter, Thomas **238**
Hunter, William 57, 277
Hunter, William Jones **238**
Hurst, Phebey **124**
Hurst, Richard 60, 61, 270, 359, 360, 404
Hurst, Richard H. 243, 270, 299, 300, 302, 352, 368, 393, 400, 412, 414, 441, 453
Hurst, Richard Hawkins **275**
Hurst, Sarah **227**
Hutchings, John **155**, 319
Hylton, William 261, **458**
Irvin, ___ 201
Irvin, Bedford 227
James, ___ Capt. 14
Jameson, David 16
Jarvis, Richard 489
Jenkins, Henry 18, **51**, 95, 183, 201, 211, 224, **245**, 298, **350**, 359
Jenkins, John 224
Jenkins, Rosea 183, 224
Jennings, Ann **409**
Jennings, Charles 28, **33**, 50, 52, 75, 79, 86, 98, 101, 115, 131, **148**, **154**, **155**, 171,

Elizabeth City County, Virginia 1787-1800

    204, 227, 235, 258, **266**, 288, 320, **339**,
    344, 347, 349, 368, 372, 392, **409**, 411,
    416, 417, 424, 431, 432, 438, 442, 453,
    489, 527, 528
Jennings, Elizabeth 154
Jennings, John 4, **137**, **154**, 185, 218, 251,
    344, **347**, 351, 363, **402**, 469
Jennings, Mary **266**
Jennings, Polly Ellmore 266
Jennings, Sarah **266** (of Norfolk)
Jennings, Thomas 148, **154**
Jennings, Thomas, Jr. **4, 34**
Jennings, William 81, 148, **154**, 216, 217, 218,
    266, 280, 320, 436
Jennis, Polly 380
Jervis, Elijah **407**
Jervis, George 227
Jervis, Susannah **407**
Jigett, ___ 99
Jigetts, Thomas **269, 478**
Jiggetts, Elizabeth 478
Jiggetts, Polly 478
Johnson, James **37**
Johnson, Priscilla **311**
Jones, ___ Mr. 141
Jones, ___ Mrs. 147, 235
Jones, Amelia **214, 296**
Jones, Anne 126, **214, 296**
Jones, Barbara **214**, 238, **258, 452**, 464
Jones, Charles 155, 161, 234, 255, 292, 307,
    360, 362, 496
Jones, Elizabeth **214**
Jones, John 170, 452
Jones, Morris 14
Jones, Rachel **14, 24**, 211, 380, 439
Jones, Richard 478
Jones, Sarah **494**
Jones, Servant 227
Jones, Susanna Pasteur 14
Jones, Thomas 16 33, 42, 58, 66, 99, 166,
    190, 197, **214**, 238, **296**, 302, 324, **326**,
    326, 330, 348, 351, 353, 384, **385**, **393**,
    414, 519, 531
Jones, Thomas, Jr. 198, 376, **446, 494**

Elizabeth City County, Virginia 1787-1800

Kerby, Elizabeth **458**
Kerby, John 118, 247, 341, **458**
Kerby, Lucy **458**
Kerby, Richard **458**
Kerby, Sarah **458**
Kerby, Thomas 50, 52, 198, 255, 272, 280, 293, 343, **349**, 446, 527
Kerby, W. 288
Kerby, William 56, 57, 83, 106, 107, 112, 140, 198, 255, 258, 279, 305, 339, 343, 345, **349**, 359, 366, 403, **458**, 523, 526, **527**
Kerby, William Thomas 273
    ALSO SEE: Kirby
King, Ann **207, 234, 237, 488**
King, Charles 412, 465
King, Elizabeth **320, 409, 521**
King, Hannah **183, 298**
King, Hannah Herbert **521**
King, Henry 227 (Col.), 234
King, Henry Jenkins **298**
King, Jane **331** (of Prince William County)
King, John **161**, 162
King, John C. **298**
King, John Curle **320, 521**
King, John Stark **161**
King, Joshua 253, 281
King, Joshua C. **298**
King, Judith Curle **298**
King, M. 507
King, Martha **50, 164, 170,** 252, **415, 444, 445, 445**
King, Mary 142, **411**
King, Michael 1, **2**, 3, 123, 125, 198, 204, 206, **207, 234,** 261, 315, 320, 348, 366, **391,** 417, 421, 444, 445, 446, 475, 484, **488,** 505, 508, 510, 515
King, Miles 7, 11, **12**, 16, **18**, 23, **25**, 29, 31, 33, **46, 50, 52,** 56, 63, 65, 66, 78, **83,** 86, 97, **98, 98,** 99, **99,** 100, 101, 102, 106, **107, 107,** 110, **112,** 124, 130, **132, 133,** 137, **139, 155, 162, 164, 170,** 175, **178,** 179, **189,** 198, **209,** 216, 226, 235, **248,** 249, **252,** 255, 269, 272, 273, **279,** 285, 286, 287, 291, 292, 296, 297, 302,

135

Elizabeth City County, Virginia 1787-1800

    305, **314**, **319**, 323, 324, 325, **327**, **330**,
    335, **336**, 337, 342 (Capt.), 349, 359, 366,
    369, **372**, 380, **389**, 391, 392, 392, **393**,
    403, **412**, **414**, **415**, 417, 420, 432, 436,
    440, 442, **443**, **446**, **449**, 451, **452**, 454,
    460, **462**, **464**, **464**, **465**, **466**, 468, **471**,
    474, 486, 489, 491, **493**, 496, 504, 506,
    508, **511**, 515, 526, 527, 527, 528
King, Rachael 391
King, William 25, 48, 95, 142, 183, 285, 286,
    297, **298**, **320**, 426, 430, 460, 469, 496,
    507, 521, 528
King, William Jr. 168, **183**, 205, 255
Kirby, John 227, 233, 489
Kirby, William 16, 170
    ALSO SEE: Kerby
Lacklin, Ann **57**
Lacklin, Philip M. **57**
Laine, John 275
Landrum, Jno. 515
Landrum, Robert **508**
Landrum, William 366, 391, 421, 508, 515
Landry, William 78
Lane, John 217, 218, 359
Lane, W. 327
Langhorn, _____ Col. 101, 417
Langhorne, Maurice 84, 492
Langhorne, William 84, **492**
Langhorne, William, Sr. **492**
Langley, Wilson 227
Langston, Matthew 227, 324
Laport, Benjamin 65
Latimer, Ester Whiten **326**
Latimer, Euphan **202**
Latimer, George 14, 29, **123**, **172**, 336, 359,
    384, 426, 473, 489, 504, 528
Latimer, James **12**, **179**, 231, 297, 360, **364**,
    372, 389, 414, **467**, **477**, 513
Latimer, John 14, 96, **172**, 253, 280, 281, 309,
    515
Latimer, Martha 54
Latimer, Mary 128, **172**
Latimer, Rosea **14**
Latimer, Sarah **326**

Elizabeth City County, Virginia 1787-1800

Latimer, Thomas 14, 28, 61, 75, 77, 97, **172**, **202**, 226, 289, 309, **326**, 336, 371, 390, 409, 436, 460
Latimer, William 7, 14, 48, 54, 72, **97**, 98, 136, 168, 188, 260, 308, 329, **336**, **337**, **426**, 430, **453**, 473, 489, 504, **512**, 526
Latimer, William Jr. 168, 260, **326**, 360, 496
Latimer, William Sr. **123**, **188**, **326**, 496
  (Above listing also includes Lattimer and Lattermore)
Latues, H. G. 438
Latues, Mary 438
Lawson, Thomas William 216
Lee, Catherine 109
Lee, Henry (Governor of Virginia) 160
Lee, William Charles **95**, **109**
Letuz, Henry Gerace 385
Letuz, M. K. 385
Lewellen, James 101
Lewis,, _____ 336
Lewis, Ann **136**
Lewis, Elizabeth **136**
Lewis, Jane **136**
Lewis, John 87
Lewis, Matthew 157, 158
Lewis, Sarah **136**
Lewis, Thomas 72, 130, **157**, 158, 360
Lewis, William 72, **136**, **157**, **158**, 329
Lewis, William Jr. **136**
Lilley, Thomas 227
Littlepage, Ralph 380
Lively, _____ Mrs. 7, **522**
Lively, David 64
Lowry, John **88**, 227
Lowry, Robert 369, 515
Lowry, Thomas 234, 369, 371, 409, 460
Lowry, William 299, 300, 369, 491, 506
Lucas, Robert 227
Lunsford, Sarah **376**
Mackintosh, Richard 227
Maddisson, James (Rev.) [Bishop of Virginia] **15**
Madison, James 182 (President of William and Mary)

Elizabeth City County, Virginia 1787-1800

Mallicote, Thomas 227
Mallory, ____ Mrs. 531
Mallory, Charles 116, 389, 438
Mallory, Edward 133, **205**
Mallory, Elizabeth 116
Mallory, Elizabeth King 252
Mallory, Francis **101**, **116**, 252, **431** (Col.), **436** (Col.), **438**, **501**
Mallory, James G. 205
Mallory, Johnson **64**, 72, **205**, 360, 371, 376
Mallory, Mary **116**, 345, 431, **432**, **436**, **438**
Mallory, Molly 431
Mallory, Rachel **64**, 145, **205**
Mallory, William 50, 52, 118, 292, 417, 446, 458, **501**
Maney, Alexander 100, 362, 509
Maney, Robert 100, 123, 342, 362, 456, 484
Manice, Grace Elizabeth 280, **280**, **281**
Manice, William **183**, 280, **280**, **281**, **308**, 360
Maniss, ____ Mrs. 496
Manniss, William 253
Manson, ____ 202
Manson, James 185, 218, 363, 469
Manson, Peter **419**, 439
Marchant, Sarah **353**
Marrow, Mary **458**
Marrow, Robert 221, 292, 391, **475**, **476**, **506**, 508, **510**, 515
Marrow, William 31, 101, 227, **458**
Marshall, Elizabeth 41
Marshall, Euphan **97**, 102
Marshall, James **97**, **115**, 489
Marshall, Martha **119**
Martin, Anthony (Doctor of Portsmouth) **109**
Mason, Elizabeth 31
Massenburg, Catherine 191
Massenburg, George 38, 39, 40, 130, 334
Massenburg, Josiah 191, 227, **324**, 489
Massenburg, Robert 55

May, James 227
McCan, ____ Mrs. 385
McCan, James Drew (of Henrico County) **143**
McCan, Sarah 144

Elizabeth City County, Virginia 1787-1800

McClurg, _____ Dr.   29
McClurg, _____ Mrs.   528
McClurg, James Dr.   380
McClurg, Rachel   **331**
McGregor, William   101
McIntosh, Richard   227
McKay, John   50
Mead, _____   344
Mead, David   143
Meade, David   145
Mehollon, John   225
Mercer, Adam (of Nansemond County)   **99**
Mercer, James   66
Meredith, Elizabeth   **173, 356**
Meredith, Elizabeth Margaret   **383, 526**
Meredith, Joseph   7, 8, 65, **69**, 71, 96, 137, **169, 173, 194**, 266, 294, 313, **356, 383, 416**, 439, **526**
Meredith, Samuel   231
Mholon, Mary   55
Mholon, William   55
Mindham, Ann   96
Mindham, Elizabeth   96
Minnis, Callohil   100, 227
Minnis, Charles   227
Minnis, Francis   102
Minson, Ann   **28**, 33, **75, 77, 131**
Minson, Banister   227, 369
Minson, George   24, 66, 179, **339**
Minson, John   68, 221, **284**, 285, **452**, 493, 499
Minson, Mary   194, **305**
Minson, Rebecca   **283**
Minson, Thomas   5, **28**, 82, 87, 100, **107, 131**, 202, 255, 282, 287, 400, **412,** 436, 474, 514
Minson, Thomas Jr.   **33, 75, 77, 98**, 140, 148, 202, **462**
Minson, William   194
Mitchell, Abraham   201
Mitchell, John   201
Mitchell, Priscilla   **126**
Mitchell, William   29 194, 227
Moore, _____ Mrs.   227
Moore, A.   29

139

Elizabeth City County, Virginia 1787-1800

Moore, Ann(e) **237, 353**
Moore, Ann Mallory 448
Moore, Augustine 98, **125**, 227, **237**, 255, **261**,
    324, 338, **353**, 420, 436, **461**, 489
Moore, Augustine Jr. 50, 56, 84, **125**, 198,
    237, 338, 353, 366, 448, 461, **488**
Moore, Augustine Sr. 125, 515
Moore, Hugh Jr. 88
Moore, Jno. 56
Moore, John **50, 52**, 197, **237**, 261, 276, 353,
    362, **366**, 444, **448**
Moore, M. 123
Moore, Mary **261**, 353
Moore, Mary Shield Hollier **366**
Moore, Merritt 227, **237**, 345, 385, **448**, **461**,
    507, 508
Moore, W. 267, 272, 273, 276
Moore, William **3**, 21, 116, 125, **127, 128**, 207,
    237, 255, **261**, 318, 320, **353**, **366, 448**,
    460, 461, 469
Moreland, Mary 31
Morris, Ann 349, **447**
Morris, B. Sheppard 349
Morris, Baldwin 119
Morris, Baldwin Shephard **477**
Morris, Chester 496
Morris, Richard **481**
Moses, Sheldon 111, 116, 377
Moss, _____ Mrs. 227
Moss, Edward 227
Moss, Francis **221**
Moss, John 380
Moss, Shelden 7, 25, 255, 320, 373, 374, 377
Mossom, Margaret 270
Muray, David **403**
Nathaniel, Susannah **247**
Naylor, _____ 164, 209
Naylor, James 369
Needham, _____ Mr., 471
Needham, John 280
Needham, Joseph 14, 24, 79, 101, 115, 142,
    164, 227, 234, 285, 286, 293, 331, 417,
    489
Negroes: Aaron 1; Abby 108; Abraham 105,

140

Elizabeth City County, Virginia 1787-1800

116; Adronus 168; Africa 486; Agnes 409; America 150; Amey 112; Amy 14, 24; Andeen 258; Andrew 286, 333, 334; Anna 168; Antoine 168; Antony 453; Argile 211; Beck 88, 253 and child, 411 and child Sally, 525; Ben 86, 116, 184, 272, 363, 461, 469, 481; Berry 116; Bess 253 and 3 children; Betty 29, 116, 238, 253, 339, 438, 440; Big Beck 111 and child, 286 and child; Bill 116; Billy 24, 116, 134, 141, 304, 311, 438; Bob 116, 253, 286, 486; Bridget 473, 528 Caleb 60, 183, 253, 280, 281, 308; Caroline 142; Casolina 168; Casear 83, 464, 488; Cate 86, 105, 438; Cato 88; Change 176; Charles 24, 86, 88, 101, 286, 309, 380; Charlotte 151, 211, 272; Chelcey 438; Chelsea 105, 116; Chelsey 473; China 1; China Lucy 1; Clabourne 167; Claiborn 64; Colley 505, 506, 515; Colly (male) 107; Cuff 252, 528; Cuffy 473; Dan 339, 431; Daniel 325, 464; Dann 238; Daphne 112; David 438, 489; Davy 116, 333, 334, 380; Deb 116; Delphia 284; Dianna 406; Diasy 481; Dick 416, 464; Dinah 62, 366, 409; Diner 453; Dolly 24, 473, 528; Emmanuel 151; Esther 366, 372, 380; Fan 1; Fanar 88; Fanny 142, 240, 253, 258, 304, 431, 489; Fener 258; Fillis 409, 473 (and child); Flax 88; Florah 366; Frances 273; Frank 88, 325, 416, 453, 514; George 24, 86, 106, 247, 286, 309, 325, 380, 416, 453, 464, 488, 505, 506, 515, 525; Gift 258; Grace 24, 304, 325, 486, 519; Grisdal 1; Gum 1; Hammard 88; Hampton 19, 30, 311, 525; Hanah 154; Hannaball 116; Hannah 63, 86, 105, 108, 116, 253 (and 3 children), 311, 325, 380, 438, 440, 464, 481, 525; Hanner 290; Hariot 438; Harry 108, 115, 216; Hester 151 (and child); Isaac 486; Isom 506; Jack 14, 24, 46, 58, 111, 116, 154, 247, 253, 290, 298, 351, 464 (the blacksmith), 473, 525, 528; Jacob 88,

Elizabeth City County, Virginia 1787-1800

115, 325, 409; James 105, 116, 214, 273, 286, 326, 406, 409, 438, 473; Jamy 216; Jane 168, 273; Jeffory 111; Jeffrey 126; Jeffry 24; Jefry 290; Jem 481; Jenny 88, 150, 304, 308, 384, 519, 525; Jeofry 253; Jerry 464; Jill 464; Jesse 60, 183, 280, 308; Jim 14, 24, 93, 416; Joan 283, 284; Joe 88, 126, 135, 141, 247, 252, 304, 380, 416, 505, 506, 515; John 409, 438, 519; John Matthew 409; Johnny 116; Johny the elder 102; Johny the younger 102; Jolly 116; Joseph 168; Jubiter 464; Judea 105 (and children), 116; Judith 211 (and children), 240, 376; Judy 105 (and children), 247, 290, 366, 438; Jupiter 283, 284, 286, 304; Kate 238, 283, 284, 438, 468; Kitty 115; Lancaster 63, 525; Lea 115; Lee 105; Lender 126 (and children); Lettice 46, 440; Lewis 116, 216, 252, 380; Lidia 105, 116; Little Fanny 111, 253; Little George 258; Liza 290; Lockey 111, 253; London 486; Louisia 168; Lucey 135, 141, 438; Luckey 438; Lucy 24, 29, 64, 105 (and children), 109, 116, 167, 258, 488; Luke 88; Lum 523; Lydia 142, 150, 247; Mall 176; Mallica 88; Manuel 24, 105, 116, 525; Maria 440; Mary 116, 142, 155, 473, 528; Matilda 273, 384; Matt 60, 116, 217; May 167; Miles 416; Mill 258; Milla 519; Milly 41, 88, 111, 253, 284, 380; Minerva 238, 339; Mingo 290, Minon 115; Moll 63, 154, 214, 304, 380; Molly 1, 29; Moses 30, 78, 438; Mossom 253; Mun 105, 116, 286 , 438; Murria 473; Murryear 88; Nan 1, 140, 273, 384, 409, 514, 528; Nancy 105 (and children), 109, 116 (and child), 298, 383, 419, 486, 506, 515; Nanney 135; Nanny 141, 246, 273, 290, 380, 473, 505; Natt 24, 88, 135, 141; Ned 102, 116, 154, 253, 258, 272, 304, 409, 438; Nelly 116 (and children), 431, 488; Neptune 155; Norfolk 88; Old Abram 7; Old Ben 60; Old Dick 515; Old

Elizabeth City County, Virginia 1787-1800

Ester 88; Old Fanny 464; Old Hannah 116, 438; Old Jack 304; Old Jenny 411; Old Jubiter 464; Old Judy 333, 334; Old Nanny 88, 384; Old Peter 253; Old Sarah 438, 481; Olive 112; Pat 253; Patcher 473; Patience 525; Patt 20, 87, 107 (and children); Patty 86, 115, 325, 505, 506, 515; Pebby 438; Peg 284, 380, 488; Pegg 102, 290, 409, 491 (and child); Peggy 116, 486; Pender 366; Penlen 14; Peter 24, 116, 154, 253, 325, 366, 409, 431, 438; Peter Bean 464; Phebe 464, 469; Pheby 24; Phill 134, 141; Phill, Jr. 135; Phillis 111, 253, 491 (and children); Phobe 60, 366; Phoebe 184, 363; Pluto 83; Plymouth 272; Pompey 493; Poplar 273; Portshire 528; Priscilla 486; Rachael 24, 64, 86, 88, 105 (and child), 115, 116, 150, 167, 253, 272, 284, 290, 376, 438, 448, 461, 525; Rodey 416; Roger 115; Rose 115, 116, 142, 150, 416, 464, 473, 528; Rubin 286; Ruth 489; Sal 111; Sall 88, 416, 462; Sally 253, 258 (and children), 307, 339 (and child), 438; Sam 88, 105, 116, 130, 135, 141, 154, 253, 258, 304, 333, 334, 409, 440, 473, 477, 528; Sampson 1; Samuel 115; Sarah 1, 46, 88, 105 (children), 116 (and children), 154, 253 (and child), 325, 441, 528; Sary 473; Silpha 102, 116; Silvia (and child) 491; Silvy 116, 416; Soney 88; Suckey 216; Sue 88, 102, 253 (and children), 333, 380 (and children), 409, 438; Sylvia 62, 183, 253, 280, 281, 308; Tea 86; Terry 63; Thaner 29; Tiller 290, 406; Tim 126, 366; Tom 29, 64, 88, 116, 167, 273, 284, 416, 438, 505, 506, 515; Toney 416; Tuber 88; Venus 29, 430, 488; Viner 86, 115; Violet 298, 339; Whitty 176; Wildley 111; Wiley 253; Will 102, 134, 141, 154, 155, 246, 438, 440, 473, 489; Wiltshire 461; Winney 272; Yellow Bob 111; Zilphan 438

Elizabeth City County, Virginia 1787-1800

Nelson, ____ General 227
Nelson, Hannah 15a
Nelson, John 15a
Nelson, Thomas 227
Nettles, ____ Mr. 362
Nettles, John 111, 436
Nettles, Ocarious 474, 528
Newell, James 109
Newsome, William 185
Newton, Thomas Jr. 375
Nichols, Joseph 23, 341
Nicholson, ____ Mr. 101
Nicholson, John 407
Nicholson, Jno. 407, 430, 451, 454, 498, 507
Nicholson, Thos. 407
Norton, John H. 227
Oswald, ____ 201, 331
Ottley, Ann **307**
Ottley, Coverton **307**
Ottley, Elizabeth **307**
Ottley, James **307**
Ottley, John **307**
Ottley, Samuel **307**
Ottley, Thomas **307**
Owings, Elizabeth **298**
Page, Elizabeth **385** 438
Page, John (of Matthews County) **145**, **252**, 279, 280, 344, 347, **377**, **385**, 438, 465
Paine, Dorothy **300**, **355**
Paine, Richard **480**
Paine, Thomas **58**, **300**, **355**, 359, 360
Parcell, Philip **124**
Parish, David 489
Parish, Edward 227
Parish, Elizabeth **62**
Parish, John 13, 56, 154, **267** (pilot), **276**, 309, 317
Parish, John Jr. **62**
Parish, Mark **62**, **270**, 525
Parish, Rebecca 489
Parish, Saley 154
Parish, William **62**, 213, **270**, 405
    ALSO SEE: Parrish
Parker, Job 526

Elizabeth City County, Virginia 1787-1800

Parriott, William 227
Parrish, John, Jr. 4
Parrish, John, Sr. 436
   ALSO SEE: Parish
Parsons, James **166**, 503, 531
Parsons, Jenny 237, 325
Parsons, John 7, 50, **70**, 247 (Capt.), 277
Parsons, Jno. **491**
Parsons, Major 391, 506
Parsons, Mary **70**, 237
Parsons, Roscow 237, 488
Parsons, Sarah 277
Parsons, Thomas **277** (of Williamsburg)
Parsons, W. A. T. 21, 123
Parsons, William 52, 436, 530
Parsons, William A. Thos. 2, 3, **70**, 155, 198,
   207, 261, 318, **475**, **476**, **491**, 505, 508,
   515
Pasteur, Blovet **45**, **110**, 185, 211, 213, 218,
   249, 358, 363, 380, 405, 469
Pasteur, Charles 363
Pasteur, Elizabeth **213**, 380, **405**
Pasteur, Susanah **45**, **110**
Patrick, Curtis 227
Patrick, Thomas 324
Pauls, John **37**, **352**, 359
Pauls, Robert **352**
Pauls, Sarah **37**
Payne, Thomas **242**, 491
Pear, Thomas 38
Pearce, Thomas **81**, 130
Pearce, William 360
Pennock, William 526
Perry, ____ Mr. 141
Perry, John 7, 15a, 24, 29, 37, 48, 66, 126,
   130, 161, 169, 170, 173, 217, 309, 324,
   417, 436, 528
Pesceed, Thomas 227
Phillips, John 474
Pickett, Abraham 513
Pierce, David (of Norfolk) 423
Pierce, Peter 227
Pierce, William 171, 185, 217, 218, 225, 290,
   319, 392, 436, 496, 504, **507**, 528

Elizabeth City County, Virginia 1787-1800

 ALSO SEE: Pearce
Pigot, Ralph 109
Plume, William 144
Pollard, Benjamin **213** (of Norfolk)
Pool, Fanny 360
Pool, Francis **360**
Pool, Jane **10**
Pool, John **10, 11, 211**, 360, 439, **465**
Pool, Robert **87**
Poole, ____ 467
Poole, Mary **179** (Of Norfolk County)
Poole, Robert 158
Poole, Robert, Sr. **179** (of Norfolk County)

Powell, ____ Dr. 227
Powell, Benjamin 106
Powell, Elizabeth (of Amherst County) **231**
Powell, Lucas (of Amherst County) **231**
Powell, Mary **126**
Powell, William 31
Prentis, Joseph **139**
Presson, Catlohill 70
Presson, John 362
Presson, Robert 139
Price, William 33, 39, 56, 515
Proby, Mary 383
Proby, Minson 56, 143, 144, **147**, 155, 279, 280, 383
Proby, Minson T. 251, 318, 353, 416
Proby, William 185
Purdie, George 227, **531**
Purdie, George Jr. 151, **233** (of York County), 341, 377, **481**
Purkinton, ____ Mrs. 302
Randle, Ann **119**, 141, **220**
Randle, Elizabeth **220**
Randle, Elizabeth Frazier **119**
Randle, James **119**, 141
Randle, John **119**, 141, 141, **220**, 362, 419, 491, 506
Randle, John Jr. 488
Randle, Mary **220**
 (INCLUDES: Randel)
Randolph, Beverly (Governor of Virginia) 2, 3

Elizabeth City County, Virginia 1787-1800

Randolph, George   439
Reade, Elizabeth (of Halifax County)   233
Reade, H.   152, 233
Reade, Hankins   **227**
Reade, John   **227**, **341**
Reade, Robert (of Halifax County)   233, **341**
Reade, Robert Sandefer (of Halifax County)   **152**
Reade, William   227
    ALSO SEE: Reid
Redman, Isaac (of Shelburn, Nova Scotia)   **14**, **24**
Redman, Susanna Pasteur   **24**
Redwood, William   285, 286, **287**
Reid, Hawkins   101
Reid, John   31, 101
    ALSO SEE: Reade
Riddlehurst, Elizabeth   **126**
Riddlehurst, F.   29
Riddlehurst, Francis   **64**, **126**, 155, **311**, 319, 436, 494
Ridley, Behathland   227
Ridley, Gerrard   227
Ridley, Peter   43, 45, 71
Roberts, John   190, 218
Roberts, Richard   227
Roberts, Samuel   227
Roberts, Thomas   227
Roberts, Thomas P.   522
Robinson, Cole   233, 341
Robinson, Edward   **481**
Robinson, Everard   151, 449
Robinson, Henry   **154**, **339**
Robinson, Jean   **154**
Robinson, John   143, 289, **304**, **339**, 377, 417, 489, 531
Robinson, Judith   **247**
Robinson, M. M.   449
Robinson, Starkey   227, 255, 380, 458, 474
Robinson, Starkey Jr.   118
Robinson, Thomas   **151**, **154**, 233, 307, 449, 472, 478, 481, 510
Roeland, ____   405
Rogers, ____ Capt.   528
Rogers, John   7, 14, 41, 69, 93, 97, **109**, 155,

Elizabeth City County, Virginia 1787-1800

    183, 185, 194, 211, 253, 281, **317**, 318, 343, 363, **375**, 380, 392, 423, 467, 469, 474, 504
Rogers, William 227
Roper, Randolph 474
Ross, Cheely **155, 222**
Ross, Dyannah **222**
Ross, Deannah **155**
Ross, Elizabeth **155, 222**
Ross, Euphan **155, 222**
Ross, Francis **46**
Ross, Francis, Jr. 530
Ross, Frank **222**
Ross, Jane **119**, 141
Ross, Johnson 120, **222**
Ross, Johnson Mallory **155**
Ross, Mallory **222**, 273
Ross, Martha **155**
Ross, Thomas 7, **222**
Routen, Richard 136, **329**, 512
Routten, Daniel **409**

Rowland, _____ 213
Rowland, _____ Mr. 120
Rowland, Mary **270**
Rowland, Richard 124, 253, 392, 500
Rowland, Samuel 120, **124**, 222, 383
Rowland, William 222, **270**
Rudd, _____ 344
Rudd, Benjamin 496
Rudd, Edward 211, 360, 496
Rudd, Susanah **154**
Russel, Hinde 211
Russell, Adam 51
Russell, Ann 227
Russell, Elizabeth **289**
Russell, Euphan **376**
Russell, Euphan Naylor 176
Russell, James 227
Russell, John 308, 341, 387, 403, 515
Russell, Penuel 227, 377, **481**
Russell, Rebekah 64, 140, 522
Russell, Robert L. 233
Russell, Robert Sandefer **481**, 530

Elizabeth City County, Virginia   1787-1800

Russell, Sandefer 227
Russell, William, 227
Sandefer, Elizabeth 100, 101, **323**
Sandefer, John 455
Sandefur, Mollie 323
Sandefur, Robert 100, 152, 216, **323**, 362, 377, 421, 509, 510
Sandefur, Samuel 227
Sandefur, William 100, **101**, 227
Sanders, Ann 455, 530
Sanders, James **362**
Sanders, John 362, 530
Sanders, Jno. 506
Sanders, Judy **362**
Sanders, Mary 362
Sanders, William **530**
Sanderson, James (Lord Mayor of London) 263
Sandrum, John 255
Sands, Penuel **51**, 245, 255, 350, 515
Sandy, Ermin 98
Sandy, William 14, 106, 128, 167, 211, 324, 436, 474, 528
Sans, J. 185
Saubot, John B. 225
Saunders, Ann **246**
Saunders, David 46, 55, 342, 377, **530**
Saunders, Elizabeth **246**
Saunders, James 207, 220, **246**, 515
Saunders, Judith 100
Saunders, Judy **246**
Saunders, Mary **246**, **481**
Saunders, Robert **246**
Saymour, John 7
Sclater, John 255, 341
Sclater, Mary 531
Scott, Thomas (of Warwick County) **71**
Selden, ____ Doctor 7, 51, 109, 489
Selden, Cary 4, 49, 143, 145, 162, 189
Selden, Joseph 86, 121, **124**, 231, 294, 372, 389, 423, 495
Selden, Nelly **194** (of Loudon County)
Selden, Samuel **97**, 132, 226, 270, **294**, 304, **311**, 326, 327, 360, 380, 415, 426, 439, 462, 479, **483**, 486, 489, 494, 496, **523**

Elizabeth City County, Virginia 1787-1800

   524, 528
Selden, Susanna **294**, **311**, **483**
Selden, Wilson Cary 18, **58**, **95**, 99, 122, **145**,
   194
Selden, Wilson Cary (Doctor) 10
Servant, ____ 12
Servant, Richard B. 358
Servant, Samuel **414**
Sewelling, Frankey 7
Seymour, Gerrard 7, 11, 55, 108, 120, 121,
   121, 211, **241**
Seymour, John 86, **211**, 227, 380, 463, 489
Seymour, Mary **454** (of Norfolk)
Seymour, W. 327
Seymour, William 7, 23, 101, 125, 255, 307,
   342, 530
Seymour, William Jr. 327
Shepard, ____ 145
Shepard, John 460, 512, 531
Shepherd, John 234
Shepard, Jno. 507
Sheppard, Ann 376
Sheppard, Bauldwin 75
Sheppard, John **209**, 260, 290, 327, **454**, 489,
   504
Sherrington, ____ 101
Shields, John 185
Shields, Ro. 478
Shields, Samuel **458**
Silverthorn, George **407**
Silverthorn, J. Thomas **407**
Silverthorn, John **407**
Silverthorn, Sabastian **407**
Simpson, Hannah **120**, 128
Simpson, John 383
Sinclair, Henry 201
Sinoire, P.F.A. 209
Skinner, ____ Mr. 362
Skinner, Anne **114**
Skinner, Elizabeth 66
Skinner, Ellison 324, **489**
Skinner, John 7, **13**, 20, 31, 48, 78, 100, 159,
   167, 211, 227, 255, 283, 324, 338, 360,
   373, 377, 391, 392, 436, 467, 474, 496,

Elizabeth City County, Virginia 1787-1800

    498, 499, 508, 509, **522**, 530, 531
Skinner, John Jr. 87
Skinner, John Sr. 515
Skinner, Rosey **114**
Skinner, Sally 31
Skinner, Samuel 284
Skinner, Thomas **31**, **114**, **495**, **413**
Skinner, William 194, 335
Skinner, Willis 66, 452
Skyrene, Henry 189
Skyrin, ____ Mr. 141
Skyrin, Henry 179, 184
Smallwood, Mary Beverly **191** (of Norfolk County)
Smelt, ____ Mrs. 7
Smelt, Cinthia 515
Smelt, David 7, 57, 255, **350**, 506, 515
Smelt, David Jr. 515
Smelt, James 391, 492, 506
Smelt, John **7**
Smelt, Joseph 7
Smelt, Miles 7, 506
Smelt, Robert 7, **107**, **220**, 362, **475**, **505**, **506**, **510**, **515**
Smelt, Wm. 515
Smith, B. 141, 255
Smith, Basill 352
Smith, Elizabeth **26**, **120**
Smith, Fanny **120**, **383**
Smith, J. 54, 58, 63, 423
Smith, James 143, 144, 169, 173, 241, 266, 302, **331**, 359, 366, 393
Smith, John 466
Smith, Joseph 100
Smith, Lawrence 227
Smith, Mary **120**, **383**
Smith, Rachel **331**
Smith, Richard H. **120**, 124, 493, 503
Smith, Samuel 498
Smith, T. 113
Smith, Thomas **1**
Smith, William **15a**, 24, **26**, 50, 56, 65, **120**, 130, 166, 175, 197, **216**, 241, 250, 339, 385, 436, 442, 493

Elizabeth City County, Virginia 1787-1800

Smithe, Richard 222, 255
Speers, David 175
Spooner, John 383, 468
Spooner, John J. 526
Spriggy, Corbin 525
Spruce, David 289, 362, 380, 510
Stevens, John 227
Stevenson, ____ Mr. 362
Stevenson, William 227
Stores, Benjamin 25, **28**, 72, 98, 282, 360
Stores, Charles **77**, **107**, **282**, **287**, 360, 504
Stores, Frasher, Jr. 99
Stores, Frazer **134**, **141**, **141**
Stores, Frazer, Jr. 77
Stores, Frazier **119**, **392**
Stores, James **291**
Stores, John 28, **282**, **287**
Stores, William 99, 282, 360, **483**
Street, Benjamin **313**
Stuart, Charles **519**
Stuart, Elizabeth **519**
Stuart, Helen Wray **519**
Stuart, Jacob Wray **519**
Stuart, John A. **519**
Stuart, Nancy Wray **519**
Sweeney, George 436
Sweney, Jane **237**
Tabb, ____ Mr. 141
Tabb, Henry 220, **250**, **325**, 331, 377, 505, 506, 515, 531
Tabb, John 175, 228, **325**, **512**
Tabb, Johnson 23, 29, 36, 100, 111, 138, 155, **250**, 277, 324, **325**, 380, 417, 436, 442, 475, 528
Tabb, Mary 125, 250, **325**
Tabb, Mary Harwood **250**
Tabb, Priscilla **325**
Tabb, Thomas 7, **325**

Taner, John 42
Tarrant, Carter 4
Tarrant, Cesar **130**, 275, **387**, 424
Tarrant, Elizabeth **439** (of Norfolk)
Tarrant, Francis 4, **439** (of Norfolk)

Elizabeth City County, Virginia 1787-1800

Tarrant, Liddy **387**
Tarrant, Lucy **109**
Tarrant, Mary **297**
Tarrant, Nancy **109**, **387**
Tarrant, Sampson **387**
Tazwell, John 227
Tennis, Aaron 451, **454**, 531
Tennis, Abraham **451**, **454** (of York County)
Tennis, Joshua **451**, **454** (of York County)
Thomas, Cornelius 185, 218, 363, 375, 469
Thomas, George 38, 39, 40
Thomas, Levi **513**
Thomas, Samuel 31, 123, 324, **421**, 449, **456**, 472, 484, 509
Thomas, Sarah **421**, **456**
Thomas, William 13
Thomas, William Ap. 221
Tinsley, Peter 528
Tompkins, ___ Mrs. 506, 515
Tompkins, James 289, **338**, **391**
Tompkins, Mary **220**
Toomer, Ann **311**, 383
Toomer, Jno. **214**, 227
Trigg, Ann **48**
Trowbridge, Sarah 251
Tucker, Anthony 66
Tucker, Curle 15
Tucker, S. G. 182 (Prof. of Law and Police, William & Mary)
Tucker, William 16
Turnbull, James 96, 133, 515
Turnbull, Mary 133
Umphlet, Thomas **68**
Vaughan, Samuel 429
Vaughan, William 479
Wager, William 7, 31, 227, 314
Walker, ___ 145
Walker, George 11, 141, **409**
Walker, John 343, 344, **402** (of Kentucky)
Walker, Patrick **449**, **502**
Wallace, ___ Mr. 31
Wallace, Catherine **267**, **276**, **317**, **366**
Wallace, Elizabeth C. 339
Wallace, James 471

Elizabeth City County, Virginia 1787-1800

Wallace, James Westwood **25**, **56**, 164
Wallace, Martha 113, 188
Wallace, Robert 7, 25, 113, 122, 164, 188, 369, 471, **472**, **474**, **528**
Wallace, Wilson 14, **84**, 113, **276**, 311, 436, 500
Wallace, Wilson C. **188**, **267**, **317**, **471**, 503
Wallace, Wilson Curle **366**
Waller, ____ Mr. 227
Waller, Benjamin 227
Ward, J. (Doctor) 496, 506
Ward, John James (of England) **184**, 363, **469**
Ward, Mary Courtney **469**
Warde, Hezekah 423
Warriner, Edmond 109
Warwick, William 231
Wash, Thomas (of Louisa County) **224**
Watkins, Elizabeth 101
Watkins, Polly 392
Watkins, Robert 214, 392
Watkins, William 11, 37, 213, 331, **392**
Watts, ___ 164
Watts, Euphan 376
Watts, Jane **122**, **172**, **176**
Watts, Jane Naylor **371**
Watts, Jean **376**
Watts, Samuel 28, 72, 145, 272, 273, 349, **376**, **409**, 419, 489, 521
Watts, Samuel Jr. **122**, 171, 326, 344, 347, 376
Watts, Samuel Sr. **122**
Watts, Thomas 33, 75, 134, 141, 141, **148**, 172, **349**, **404**, **409**, 443, 489
Webb, Armiger 31
Webb, Daniel 477
Webster, Thomas 227
Wellings, Elizabeth **206**
Wellings, John **492**, 508
Wellings, Thomas **206**, 360
Wellings, Robert **9**
   ALSO SEE: Willings
Wells, Matthew 227
West, Thomas **324**
Westwood, ____ Capt. 23
Westwood, ____ Col. 7, 100, 102, 141, 442, 491

Elizabeth City County, Virginia 1787-1800

Westwood, Hannah **138, 243,** 315, **388, 404**
Westwood, John S. 331, 368, 411
Westwood, Jno. L. 404, **494,** 510, 519, 526, 528
Westwood, John Stith 142, 171, **235,** 269, **279,** 285, 286, **287,** 492
Westwood, Judith 142
Westwood, Merrit 31, 279
Westwood, W. 255, 427
Westwood, William 201, **235, 279,** 500
Westwood, Worlick **2, 3,** 5, 15a, **37,** 43, 50, 52, **56, 61,** 70, **81, 82,** 95, 99, **123, 138, 139,** 165, **175, 211,** 227, **234, 243, 248,** 275, 291, 305, 313, **315,** 317, 323, 330, **331,** 356, **358,** 359, 368, **388, 404,** 405, **427, 438,** 442, 474, 486, 493, 494, 515, **528**
Westwood, Worlick Jr. 400, 404, 412, 427, **438,** 465, 466
Weymouth, ___ Mrs. 289, 510
Weymouth, Anne **134**
Weymouth, John 5, **134,** 442, 456, 481, 493
Whitaker, ___ Doctor 360
Whitaker, Armistead 83
Whitaker, Jonathan **251**
Whitaker, Nathaniel **251** (physician formerly from Canan, Mass.)
Whitaker, Sarah **251**
Whitaker, William Smith **251**
    ALSO SEE: Whittaker
White, Charles 426
Whitfield, Hanes 33
Whittaker, Rebecca **427**
    ALSO SEE: Whitaker
William & Mary College Masters & President **182**
Williams, ___ Dr. 489
Williams, Ann **72**
Williams, Cale James 10
Williams, Christiana 360
Williams, Frederick **161, 189**
Williams, James **290,** 474
Williams, James Waller 206, **329**
Williams, John 63, **72, 157, 158,** 292, 342, 359, **441**
Williams, Mary 16, **441**

Elizabeth City County, Virginia 1787-1800

Williams, Nancy **441**
Williams, Richard 304, **329**, 360, 465
Williams, Sarah **409**
Williams, William **409**, **421** (of Warwick County), 456, 484
Willings, John 255, 508, 515
Willings, Jno. 255
Willings, Robert **23**
Willings, Thomas 255
    ALSO SEE: Wellings
Wills, William S. 458
Wilson, Ann **20, 87, 246**
Wilson, James Saunders **246**
Wilson, John 7, 101, **206**, 207, 255, 291, **292**, 342, 345, 362, 417, 442, 522
Wilson, John Jr. 134, **291**
Wilson, Mary 223, 292
Wilson, Sally 487
Wilson, Willis 255, 360, 362, 436
Wise, Mary **448**
Wise, William 227
Witts, William 227
Wood, Bennett **487**
Wood, Hannah **487**
Wood, J. 227
Wood, James **38, 39, 40**, 130, 439, **487**
Wood, John 9, 101, 123, 440, **487**, 515
Wood, Lazarus 289, 292
Wood, Margaret **38**, 130
Wood, Martha **487**
Wood, Mary 206, 380, 455
Wood, Robert **487**
Wood, William **487**
Woody, Nathan 31
Wooten, Ann **48**
Wooten, Benjamin (of Smithfield) **48, 54**, 403, 489
Wooten, John **48**
Wooten, Mary **54**
Wooten, Thomas 7, **48, 54, 211**
Wooten, Thomas Jr. **493**
Wooten, William **48**
Wootten, Thomas 29, 43
Wray, ____ Mrs. 506

Elizabeth City County, Virginia 1787-1800

Wray, Ann R. **377**
Wray, Ann Rosetta **368, 384**
Wray, Dianna 116
Wray, George 15a, 63, 70, 79, 110, 116, **138, 160**, 164, 175, 201, 227, **272**, 275, **293**, 297, 313, **343, 344**, 345, **347**, 366, 376, **402**, 420, 436, 446, 480, 496, **519**, 526, 531
Wray, George, Jr. 109
Wray, Jacob 29, **70**, 124, 138, **272, 273**, 277, **293, 368, 384, 463**, 491, **519**
Wray, John 41, 70, 138, 235
Wray, John A. 58, 123, 194, 252, 270, 299, 300, 313, 344, 347, 359, 442
Wray, John Ashton **160, 273**, 288, 297, **368, 384, 519**
Wray, Mary Ann **519**
Wray, William 29
Wright, Matthew 380
Wylde, Thomas 189
Wymore, John 31
Wythe, George 118, 458
Wythe, Margaret 118, 458
Wythe, Thomas 118
Yancey, Archelaus **216, 224, 225, 260, 496**, 504, **507**
Yancey, Charles **401** (of Louisa County), 507
Yancey, David **401**, 507
Yancey, Mary **224, 225**
Yancy, Nathan 29, 436
Yancey, Polly 401
Yeargain, John 509, 515
Yeargin, _____ Mrs. 421
Young, Charles **236** (of London but sailing for Virginia)
Young, Richard 478

Elizabeth City County, Virginia 1787-1800

Elizabeth City County, Virginia 1787-1800

INDEX OF PLACES AND LANDMARKS

Alley, unnamed (in Hampton) 161
Ashton Manor 272
Averas (on Harris Creek) 426
Back River 46, 118, 179, 188, 330, 377, 451, 454, 458, 531
Back Street 57, 400
Bakers (Plantation) 486
Black Ground 330
Blacksmith Shop 348
Boutwell 326
Briar Field 84
Bridges, unnamed 279; Also see: Free School Bridge, Fox Hill Bridge, Long Creek Bridge, Naylor's Bridge, York County Bridge
Bright's Estate 171
Broad Creek 475
Buckroe Tract 145, 252
Cary's Ditch 350
Celey's Road 279
Cemetaries, unnamed: 50, 106; Also see: Fox Hill, Harris Creek
Chesapeake Bay 179 (implied), 467
Colledge (College) Land 155, 161, 173, 182, 356
Courthouse Lane 182
Coves 159, 201 (Hampton) 330 (Back River), 337 (Fox Hill), 344 (Mill Creek)
Creeks, unnamed 11, 13, 39, 40, 57, 96, 242 (Hampton), 276, 337 (Fox Hill), 364, 366; Also see: Broad Creek, Elk Horn (Kentucky), Hampton Creek, Harris Creek, Hogshead Quarter Creek, Long Creek, Mill Creek, Saltford's Creek, Slippery Pine Branch, Whitehall Creek
Dams See: Scones
Dinwiddie County 368
Eaton Free School Land 121, 276, 366
Elk Horn Creek (Kentucky) 224
Erroll 164, 460, 471
Fairfield (owned by John Creek) 15
Ferry Point 242

Elizabeth City County, Virginia 1787-1800

Fox Hill   54, 123, 136, 179, 226, 337
Fox Hill Bridge   54
Fox Hill, cemetary   179
Fox Hill Ridge   336
Fox Hill Road   (Road to Fox Hill)   34, 369
Free School   118, 236, 458 (road to)
Free School Bridge   236
Free School Swamp   236
Glebe Land   143, 231
Good Wood Plantation   175
Greenland   209, 369
Hampton Creek   171, 294, 302, 483
Hampton River   13, 39, 40, 43, 81, 82, 113, 139, 143, 170 (implied), 171, 201, 242 (Ferry Point and Irvins Point), 275, 299, 300, 331, 355 (east side), 376, 385, 465, 471, 480, 486, 494, 503
Hampton Town (also see Southampton) 13, 37, 38, 39, 40, 43, 45, 56, 57, 81, 82, 113, 130, 147, 161, 162, 169, 170, 178, 182, 185, 189, 194, 198, 211, 218, 234, 243, 266, 267, 275, 293, 294, 302, 313, 315, 318, 319, 331, 352, 356, 363, 368, 375, 376, 385, 400, 404, 423, 427, 438, 439, 469, 494
Harris Creek   48, 72, 148, 209, 329, 369, 371, 426, 497
Harris Creek, cemetary   148
Harris Creek Mill   72
Herrons   61
Hogshead Quarter Creek   54
Irvins Point   242
James River   18, 95, 99, 183
James Swamp   236
Jenkins Plantation   51
Kentucky (State of)   224
King Street   56, 161, 170, 173, 182, 243, 315, 331, 352, 356, 376, 385, 427, 438, 494
Lilliput (owned by John Creek)   15
Little England   65, 133, 249
Little Scotland   139
Long Creek   145
Long Creek Bridge   145
Low Fields   296
Luke Ridge   421

160

Elizabeth City County, Virginia 1787-1800

Main Road   18, 28, 75, 131, 164, 206, 209, 233, 236, 302, 320, 358, 420, 471, 483
Main Street (leading to wharf)   234, 313, 315
Mile (Mill) Ordinary   276, 366
Mill Creek   12, 213, 231, 270, 305, 344, 389, 405, 414, 495
Mill Marsh (Salftord's Creek   25
Mill (Mile) Ordinary   276, 366
Mill Pond (Armistead's)   492
Mills, unnamed   25 (wind), 72; Also see: Harris Creek Mill, Purdie's Mill, Read's Mill, Steven's Mill (Warwick County), Tompkins Mill, Wises Water Grist Mill
Naylor's Bridge   369
Norfolk   84
North Branch River   377 483, 531
North Street   185, 194, 204, 218, 266, 363, 423, 469
Old Field (Harris Creed)   148
Oppossum Hall   123
Ordinaries   See   Mile Ordinary, Mill Ordinary, Thompkins Ordinary
Peach Tree Field   209, 460
Pembrooke   214
Plantations: See Ashton Manor, Averas, Bakers, Black Ground, Boutwell, Briar Field, Bright's Estate, Erroll, Fairfield, Goodwood Plantation, Greenland, Herrons, Jenkins Plantation, Lilliput, Little England, Little Scotland, Low Fields, Oppossum Hall, Peach Tree Field, Pembrooke, Saltfords Creek; Unnamed: 95, 128, 143, 191, 339, 353, 456
Poack Street   113
Poquoson River   118, 458
Public Road   171
Purdie's Mill   531
Queen Street   37, 45, 147, 173, 201, 211, 315, 318, 352, 356, 375, 404
Read's Mill   502
Riddlehurst property   319
Rivers, unnamed   4, 33, 120, 164, 170, 242, 330, 415; Also see: Back River, Hampton River, James River, North Branch, Poquoson River

Elizabeth City County, Virginia 1787-1800

Roads, unnamed   70, 118, 131, 279 (crossroads), 282, 299, 300, 314, 501; Also see: Celey's Road, Fox Hill Road, Main Road, Public Road, Sawyer's Swamp Road, Warwick Road, Whiting's Road
Saltford's Creek   16, 58, 97, 269, 273, 429, 452, 454
Saltford's Creek Plantation   428
Sawpits   4 (Cowpers), 164 (Wallace's), 469 (Erroll)
Sawyer's Swamp   49, 175, 358, 497
Sawyer's Swamp Road (Road to Sawyer's Swamp)   358, 420, 446
School House   369 (south side of Harris Creek)
Scones Dam   202, 492
Slippery Pine Branch   66 (flows into Saltford's Creek)
Southampton   155, 173, 201, 204
Steven's Mill (Warwick County)   223
Streets: See Back Street, Courthouse Lane, King Street, Main Street, North Street, Poach Street, Queen Street
Swamps, unnamed   51, 72, 75, 77, 209, 279, 350, 493; Also see: Sawyer's Swamp, Free School Swamp, James Swamp
Thompin's (Thompkin's ?) Ordinary   481
Tompkin's Mill (York County)   26
Warwick County   223
Warwick Road (Road to Warwick)   203, 233, 481
Water Grist Mill   377, 502, 531
Wharf   234, 313, 315
Whitehall Creek   157
Whitings Road   10
William and Mary Colledge Land   173, 182, 356
Wine Street   194, 294, 375, 427, 439
Wise's Mill Pond   341
Wise's Water Grist Mill   341, 377
Wood Landing (Rowe Cooper)   4
York County   26, 377
York County Bridge   26

www.ingramcontent.com/pod-product-compliance
Lightning Source LLC
Chambersburg PA
CBHW050819160426
43192CB00010B/1823